CIVIL RIGHTS
STRUGGLES
around the
WORLD

WE STAND AS ONE

THE INTERNATIONAL LADIES GARMENT WORKERS STRIKE,

New York, 1909

LAURA B. **EDGE**

 TWENTY-FIRST CENTURY BOOKS ■ **MINNEAPOLIS**

Dedicated to Gerry, for his steadfast encouragement

Copyright © 2011 by Laura B. Edge

All rights reserved. International copyright secured. No part of this book may be reproduced, stored in a retrieval system, or transmitted in any form or by any means—electronic, mechanical, photocopying, recording, or otherwise—without the prior written permission of Lerner Publishing Group, Inc., except for inclusion of brief quotations in an acknowledged review.

Twenty-First Century Books
A division of Lerner Publishing Group, Inc.
241 First Avenue North
Minneapolis, MN 55401 U.S.A.

Website address: www.lernerbooks.com

Library of Congress Cataloging-in-Publication Data

Edge, Laura Bufano, 1953–
    We stand as one : the International Ladies Garment Workers Strike, New York, 1909 / by Laura B. Edge.
        p.   cm. — (Civil rights struggles around the world)
    Includes bibliographical references and index.
    ISBN 978–0–7613–4609–8 (lib. bdg. : alk. paper)
    1. Strikes and lockouts—Clothing trade—New York (State)—New York—History—20th century—
Juvenile literature. 2. Women clothing workers—New York (State)—New York—History—20th century—
Juvenile literature. 3. Women in the labor movement—New York (State)—New York—History—20th
century—Juvenile literature. I. Title.
    HD5325.C621909 .N484 2011
    331.892'88709747109041—dc22   2009049345

Manufactured in the United States of America
1 – CG – 7/15/10

CONTENTS

THE CAUSE I NOW PLEDGE

On Monday, November 22, 1909, the International Ladies Garment Workers Union held a meeting at Cooper Union, a college for working-class people in New York City. The workers who gathered on that historic evening labored in shirtwaist factories. They made blouses called shirtwaists, which women wore with floor-length skirts. The majority of shirtwaist makers were young immigrant women. Some had come to the United States from Italy. Others were Jewish women from Russia and eastern Europe.

Thousands of shirtwaist workers from factories all over the city poured into the huge brownstone building. They met in the cellar, in the Great Hall, where Abraham Lincoln had once given a stirring speech about liberty. Workers from two of the

Samuel Gompers, president of the American Federation of Labor (AFL) union, speaks to members of the International Ladies Garment Workers Union on November 22, 1909, in New York City.

largest shirtwaist factories in New York, Leiserson Shirtwaist Factory and the Triangle Waist Company (also sometimes called the Triangle Shirtwaist Company), were on strike. They had stopped working to pressure their employers to pay higher wages and to improve working conditions in factories. The workers' discontent had been building for years. According to William Mailly of the newspaper *New York Call*, their unhappiness was the result of "low wages that went lower in hard times, but never higher in good times, of long hours of day and night and Sunday labor in the busy season and idleness or semi-idleness in the dull season, of unsanitary shop conditions, with poor light, foul air and unhealthy surroundings, of the tyranny, and sometimes worse, of petty bosses and foremen... all these things had combined to make the general lot of the shirtwaist makers miserable, degrading and increasingly oppressive."

The young women at the meeting came to hear union leaders discuss the possibility of a general strike, or a strike of all shirtwaist makers in the city. Many hoped that a general strike would raise wages and improve working conditions in every shirtwaist factory in New York.

The Great Hall filled to overflowing, and union organizers turned hundreds away at the door. Organizers hastily

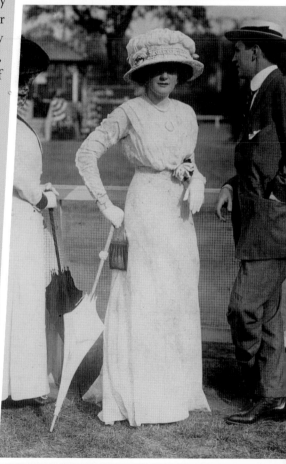

The shirtwaist blouse, coupled with a floor-length skirt, was fashionable among women in the early 1900s.

secured three additional meeting places, and workers crowded into them. And still people were turned away. They stood in the streets outside the buildings and strained to catch bits of conversation as it floated out the doors.

Mary Dreier, president of the New York Women's Trade Union League (WTUL), was the only woman scheduled to speak that November night. Among the male speakers was Samuel Gompers, president of the American Federation of Labor (AFL), the nation's leading labor organization. When Gompers rose to speak, the audience sprang to its feet and cheered for several minutes. Gompers told his audience that working conditions in the clothing trade were "a blot on modern civilization."

Gompers and the other male speakers acknowledged the poor working conditions, long hours, and low pay of the shirtwaist workers, but they stopped short of calling for a general strike. They knew that the police often arrested striking workers for disturbing the peace and sometimes roughed them up. Some strikers ended up in prison. Strikers also endured financial hardships, since they lost their paychecks when they went on strike. In addition, in this era, many men viewed women as weak and flighty. Male union leaders had little faith that women could launch and maintain a successful strike.

As the speeches continued, runners traveled back and forth between Cooper Union and the overflow halls. They delivered updates and kept the workers informed about what each speaker recommended. As the evening wore on, the crowd's enthusiasm faded. The women in the audience were ready to strike, yet the men who led the union advised caution.

After two hours of speeches, twenty-three-year-old Clara Lemlich had heard enough. Lemlich, a Jewish immigrant from a small village in Ukraine, worked at Leiserson Shirtwaist Factory. Lemlich had been striking for three months. She and her fellow strikers picketed, or marched back and forth, in front of the Leiserson factory. They urged other workers to join the strike. Leiserson's owners wanted to keep the factory operating at full production, without interference from picketers, so they called in the police. In the course of three months, Lemlich had been arrested seventeen times. The police had beaten her and broken her ribs.

Lemlich interrupted Jewish labor leader Jacob Panken as he started to speak. "I want to say a few words," she said in her native Yiddish, the language of eastern European Jews. Voices all around the hall rang out. They encouraged the young worker to get up on the platform so everyone could hear what she had to say. The women beside her lifted Lemlich onto the stage. She could barely see over the podium. "I am a working girl," she said, "one of those who are on strike against intolerable conditions. I am tired of listening to speakers who talk in general terms. What we are here for is to decide whether we shall or shall not strike. I offer a resolution that a general strike be declared—now."

Jewish workers translated Lemlich's words into English and Italian, and the meeting broke into wild applause. When meeting chair Benjamin Feigenbaum asked for a second to the motion, a chorus of seconds rang out. Women cheered, stamped their feet, and waved hats, handkerchiefs, and U.S. flags.

When Feigenbaum called for a vote, the huge gathering leaped to its feet

Clara Lemlich worked at the Leiserson Shirtwaist Factory in New York City. A Jewish immigrant, she spoke at the November 22, 1909, meeting and urged other shirtwaist workers to strike.

Women raise their hands to vote for the shirtwaist workers strike at the meeting on November 22, 1909.

once again. A resounding roar of "ayes" swept through the hall. The motion carried unanimously, and the crowd exploded with thunderous applause that lasted for several minutes.

Then Feigenbaum rapped on a table, settled down the workers, and measured their commitment. "Will you take the old Jewish oath?" he called. Thousands of right hands went up, and the audience repeated after him as one: "If I turn traitor to the cause I now pledge, may this hand wither from the arm I now raise."

Union leaders appointed a committee of fifteen women, with one young man to lead them, to poll workers at the other assembly rooms. Committee members hurried to the overflow halls and presented

the strike motion. Workers at all three meeting halls unanimously endorsed the motion.

The next morning, Tuesday, November 23, 1909, New York's shirtwaist workers reported for work as usual. At ten o'clock, a union representative in each shop gave the signal. Then, more than twenty thousand workers from five hundred factories laid down their scissors, fastened on their hats, and walked off the job.

The Uprising of Twenty Thousand, the first major strike by women in the United States, was a pivotal moment in U.S. history. But what did it really mean to young immigrant factory workers? What did it mean to the U.S. labor movement and to future generations of women?

CHAPTER 1

A
HUMAN
TIDE

When I had to quit school in the fifth grade, I felt terribly abused though I accepted it as part of life for a girl of a poor family."

—Jennie Matyas, Lower East Side immigrant and factory worker, n.d.

More than twenty-three million people moved to the United States between 1880 and 1920. The majority emigrated from southern and eastern Europe—Italy, Russia, Lithuania, Romania, Poland, Greece, and Hungary—a vast human tide. Some came to escape ethnic and religious persecution. Others came to escape crushing poverty. They hoped to find jobs and a better life and came with the feeling that anything was possible in the United States.

The immigrants traveled by sea, with many ships docking in New York City. While some immigrants continued on to other cities and towns, a large number of them stayed in New York.

Below: At Ellis Island, a major immigration station in New York City, health inspectors examine immigrants.

As their ships entered New York Harbor, immigrants passed the Statue of Liberty. Designed by French sculptor Frédéric-Auguste Bartholdi, the statue stands more than 300 feet [91 meters] high. The people of France gave the statue to the people of the United States as a symbol of friendship between the two countries. Construction began in France in 1875. In 1885–1886, U.S. workers assembled the statue in New York.

Inspired by the soon-to-be-complete statue, U.S. poet Emma Lazarus wrote the sonnet "The New Colossus" in 1883. (The old Colossus was a giant statue in ancient Greece.) The poem speaks of the statue and of the United States as welcoming to immigrants. It reads in part:

> Give me your tired, your poor,
> Your huddled masses yearning to breathe free,
> The wretched refuse of your teeming shore.
> Send these, the homeless, tempest-tost to me,
> I lift my lamp beside
> the golden door!

The Statue of Liberty in New York Harbor is a beacon of hope to immigrants crossing the Atlantic Ocean.

In 1903 workers engraved the sonnet on a bronze plaque and placed it on an inner wall of the statue's pedestal.

■ THE ITALIANS

One of the largest immigrant groups to arrive in New York during this period came from Italy. There, farmers and unskilled laborers endured many hardships. Most dwelled in tiny hillside villages, like their ancestors before them. A wealthy few owned most of the land. Landowners charged high rents and paid their peasant workers low wages. Many families who farmed the land lived in one-room hovels. They faced starvation on a daily basis.

Italian girls were expected to help with household chores and care for younger siblings. Many also worked in the fields. "When I was five or six years old, my father gave me a small scythe [cutting tool] with which to help harvest the grain," recalled an Italian peasant. "Around the fingers of my left hand my mother placed five *cannedda* [protective coverings] so that I would not cut my fingers while learning. All the girls in my village worked as I did. We also did much housework, following our mothers around continuously. There was never an idle moment for girls or women. We all wanted to earn the reputation of being good workers."

With few prospects for improving their lives in Italy, peasants and laborers came to the United States in droves. Many planned to work for a while, save their money, and return to their homeland to buy a farm, a home, or a business. Some sent money home to support their Italian relatives. Others sent money so that family members could book passage on a ship and join them in the United States.

■ THE RUSSIAN JEWS

Russian Jews were another large immigrant group. In Russia Jewish women managed their households and also worked outside the home to help support their families. Many worked in small shops or factories, sewing clothing, gloves, and other textiles. But Russia's labor market was overcrowded. The result was widespread unemployment, especially for those on the lowest rung of the employment ladder—Jewish women.

In Russia and other parts of Europe, people latched on to new political and economic philosophies. One of these was Socialism.

Jewish immigrants arrive at Ellis Island in the early 1900s. Most Jewish immigrants at that time came from Russia or eastern Europe.

Socialists thought that governments should limit private business ownership and distribute a nation's wealth equally among its citizens to bring about equality in living standards. In Russia a group of Jewish Socialists formed a Jewish workers' union, known as the Bund, and went on strike in the early 1900s. They held protest rallies to garner support for their cause, and thousands of young Jewish working women joined this movement.

Meanwhile, anti-Semitism, or discrimination against Jews, flourished in Russia. Russian Jews could live only in certain neighborhoods and hold only certain jobs. Anti-Semitic violence was widespread. Sometimes mobs of Russian peasants and soldiers slaughtered whole communities or villages of Jews.

To escape the oppression, millions of Jews traveled to port cities in Europe, boarded steamships, and emigrated to the United States. Many of these immigrants brought the ideals of Socialism and labor activism with them. Unlike their Italian counterparts, the vast majority of Jewish immigrants had no desire to return to their homeland. They came to the United States to stay and to make new lives in their adopted country.

■ A COMMON BOND

Their lives had been different in their homelands, but Italian and Jewish women shared a common cultural trait. Both groups were considered inferior to men—second-class citizens. As Italian American educator Leonard Covello recalled, "When I was about twelve years of age my father told me plainly that it was my duty to watch over my sisters. 'Son,' he would say, 'your sisters are women, just like other women. Don't give them too much liberty. Don't let them get out of hand. They are incapable of exercising any freedom.'"

The Jewish culture also valued boys more than girls. Ida Richter, an immigrant from a small town near Minsk, recalled, "In Russia, a woman was nothing. . . . When my father used to pray in the morning with his prayer shawl, I used to hear him say in Hebrew [the ancient language of Jews], 'Thank God I'm not a woman.' A girl wasn't much."

But in this era, the status of Italian and Jewish immigrant women was actually not much different from the status of all women in the United States. In the early 1900s, women did not have the right to vote. Within families, girls and women were expected to defer to their fathers, husbands, and brothers. If women worked, they were expected to turn their wages over to their families.

■ CITY LIFE

Early twentieth-century newcomers to New York City exchanged a traditional, rural way of life for the most modern city on Earth. In New York, technology was changing at a dizzying pace. Automobiles began

Above: The mansion of wealthy industrialist Andrew Carnegie sat on the corner of Ninety-first Street and Fifth Avenue in Manhattan. *Right:* In the early 1900s in New York, horses and carriages shared the streets with automobiles.

to replace horses, electric lights illuminated the streets, skyscrapers loomed like giants, and workers built the largest subway (underground railway) system in the world. For many immigrants, the adjustment was frightening and painful.

The city itself was a spectacle. New York had the busiest harbor, the longest bridges, the worst slums, and the grandest mansions. Rich industrialists lived on lavish estates and displayed their wealth with reckless abandon. Andrew Carnegie's sixty-four room, six-story mansion on the corner of Ninety-first Street and Fifth Avenue boasted the most modern features of the day. The stately home had a structural steel frame, an elevator, a huge library, and central heating. Not to be outdone, Carnegie's business partner, Henry Clay Frick, built an even more elaborate home, designed to "make Carnegie's place look like a miner's shack." Frick's marble palace held one of New York's finest art collections.

■ ■ ■ ■ THE LOWER EAST SIDE

In sharp contrast to Carnegie and Frick, newly arrived immigrants lived in extreme poverty, crowded into tenement slums. They came to New York with little or no money. Most could not speak English. The majority of newcomers crammed into the city's Lower East Side. Within this area, each ethnic group created its own community. Italians, Jews, Poles, and Greeks settled into their own neighborhoods. The Lower East Side, one of the most densely populated areas in the world, became a mosaic of ethnic neighborhoods.

Italian immigrants often settled in neighborhoods with people from the same village or city in Italy. One street might house people from Genoa; another street, immigrants from Palermo or Naples. The Italians settled around Mulberry Street on the Lower East Side and in another section of New York called Five Points.

People crowd onto Mulberry Street in New York in the early 1900s. Street vendors in this Italian neighborhood sold almost every kind of food, clothing, and household item imaginable.

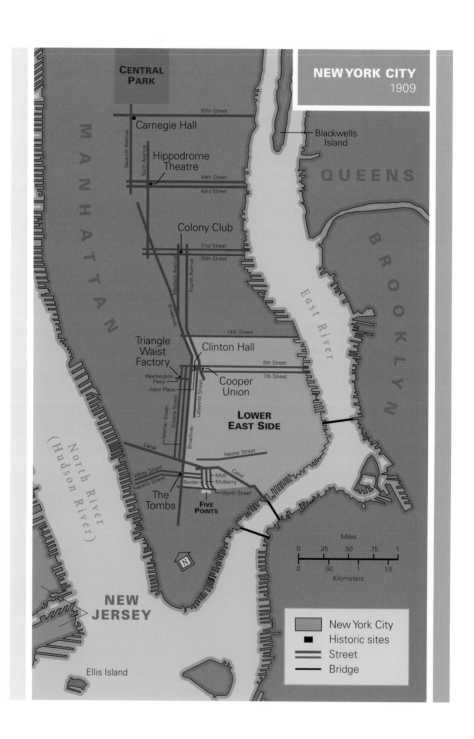

CENTRAL
PARK

NEW YORK CITY
1909

Carnegie Hall

Blackwells
Island

Hippodrome
Theatre

QUEENS

57th Street

Seventh Avenue
Sixth Avenue

44th Street

43rd Street

M
A
N
H
A
T
T
A
N

Colony Club

31st Street

30th Street

Madison Avenue
Fourth Avenue

B
R
O
O
K
L
Y
N

East River

14th Street

Triangle
Waist
Factory

Clinton Hall

8th Street

Broadway

University Place

7th Street

Washington
Place

Cooper
Union

Astor Place

Lafayette Street

LOWER
EAST SIDE

Mercer Street
Greene Street
Broadway

Canal

Hester Street

North River
(Hudson River)

White Street

Canal

Franklin Street

Mott
Mulberry

Baxter

The
Tombs

Worth Street

FIVE
POINTS

Miles

0   .25   .50   .75   1

N

0   .50   1   1.5

Kilometers

NEW
JERSEY

New York City

Historic sites

Ellis Island

Street

Bridge

Jewish immigrants revolved their community around Hester Street. The neighborhood had kosher butchers, who killed animals for food according to Jewish dietary law; synagogues, or Jewish houses of worship; bakeries that made traditional Jewish bread; Yiddish theaters; and Yiddish newspapers.

Whether they were Jewish, Italian, or another eth-nicity, most newcomers lived in tenement houses. Many of these wooden structures rose six, seven, or eight stories into the air. Each floor generally held four apartments, each consisting of two rooms. One room served as kitchen, dining room, and living room; and the other, as a bedroom. Privacy was nonexistent. Bathrooms were shared— two toilets to a floor at best or outdoor privies at worst. The apartments had few windows and poor ventilation. Immigrants used every inch of valuable space, even the air between tenement buildings, where women strung laundry to dry. High above the street, clothing fluttered in the breeze, adding to the sense of closeness and congestion.

Laundry hangs across an alley between tenement houses in New York in the early 1900s.

Small tenement apartments on the Lower East Side usually held large families, with several generations under one roof.

Most immigrants lived with extended family—grandparents, aunts, uncles, and cousins—in addition to parents and children. Many families shared their tiny apartments with boarders, or renters. The rent money provided a little extra income for the family. People slept two to a bed, on mattresses on the floor, and on boards laid between two chairs. People often slept in shifts. Those who worked at night slept during the day, and those who worked the day shift slept in the same beds at night. As one boarder recalled, on a typical day, "The cantor [synagogue singer] rehearses, a train passes, the shoemaker bangs, ten brats run around like goats, the wife putters in her 'kosher restaurant.' At night, we all try to get some sleep in the stifling, roach-infested two rooms."

A CONSTANT HUSTLE AND BUSTLE

The streets of the Lower East Side were a vast open-air market. Thousands of pushcart peddlers sold everything imaginable. Some sold food—dried fruit, fresh fruit, pickles, meat, fish, and vegetables. Others sold household utensils, jewelry, boots, and shoes. Still others sold inexpensive ready-made clothing, low-cost "dime novels," and stationery. According to a commission appointed to investigate the city's pushcarts, "When our list of goods sold was complete, we felt it would have been easier to make a list of things that were not sold."[13]

As peddlers hawked their wares, shouting in a babble of foreign tongues, women in dark skirts, shawls, and kerchiefs moved from cart to cart, searching for bargains. Children played games such as tag and jacks on the streets. At times, the din was deafening. The rattle of horse-drawn wagons mixed with the rumble of trains and the clanging of trolleys. A pungent odor hung over it all. The stench of rotting garbage mixed with the smell of horse droppings, unwashed bodies, and waste from backyard privies.

Pushcart vendors such as this man sold their goods on the streets of New York.

In part because of immigration, New York's population more than doubled between 1880 and 1910, from 1.9 million to 4.8 million people.

Despite the dirt and chaos, the city was a marvel—especially to new immigrants. Rose Cohen, a Russian Jewish immigrant, recalled her early days in New York: "I was dazed by all there was to see. I looked with wonder at the tall houses, the paved streets, the street lamps. As I had never seen a large city and only had had a glimpse of a small one, I thought these things true only of America."

TURNING INTO AN AMERICAN

Immigrant women, especially young women, wanted to become "real Americans" as quickly as possible. They wanted to look and sound American. They bought inexpensive clothing in the latest styles. They bought suits and hats. They took night classes to learn English and practiced reading with dime novels and newspapers. Sophie Abrams described her transformation into an American girl:

> My first day in America I went with my aunt to buy some American clothes. She bought me a shirtwaist, you know, a blouse and a skirt, a blue print with red buttons and a hat, such a hat I had never seen. I took my old brown dress and shawl and threw them away! I know it sounds foolish, we being so poor, but I didn't care. I had enough of the old country. When I looked in the mirror, I couldn't get over it. I said, boy, Sophie, look at you now. Just like an American.

The Lower East Side provided all kinds of entertainment for the new immigrants. They marveled at the wonders of the nickelodeon, a motion picture theater with a five-cent admission charge. After the movie, they visited ice cream parlors, soda shops, and candy stores.

SWEATSHOPS AND FACTORIES

In 1909 New York was the center of the ready-to-wear garment industry. Previously, most clothing had been homemade. But in the early 1900s, people started to buy ready-made clothing, produced in factories. The garment industry was one of the largest employers of women in the United States, and the majority of immigrant women worked as unskilled laborers in this "needle trade."

Married garment workers usually did their labor at home. They worked in the kitchen, beside the stove. In summer the heat was overwhelming. The sweltering conditions led to the nickname sweatshop for these home workshops and later for all factories in which workers toiled in poor conditions for low wages.

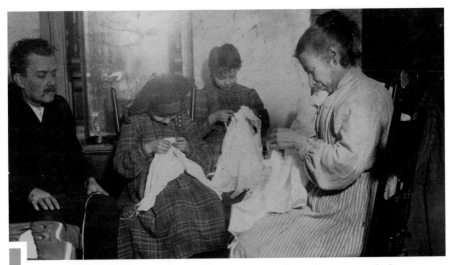

This mother and her daughters sew garments for a factory at their home in New York City in the early 1900s.

Sweatshop workers collected bundles of precut fabric, carried them home, and sewed them into clothing. Children of all ages, some as young as three, worked alongside their mothers. Sweatshop workers generally earned between three and seven dollars a week. Immigrant Abraham Cahan described a typical New York sweatshop:

> The shop was one of a suite of three rooms on the third floor of a rickety old tenement house on Essex Street, and did the additional duty of the family's kitchen and dining-room.... Bundles of cloth, cut to be made into coats, littered the floor, lay in chaotic piles by one of the walls, cumbered Mrs. Lipman's kitchen table and one or two chairs, and formed, in a corner, an impoverished bed upon which a dirty two-year-old boy ... was enjoying his siesta.

Unmarried garment workers usually worked in factories instead of homes. Child labor laws were scarce and rarely enforced in this era, so girls as young as eleven worked in factories to help support their families. Thirteen-year-old Lenore Kosloff, a Lithuanian Jew, felt obligated to work:

> I accepted my responsibility to help support my family even though this meant I wouldn't go to high school. I wanted to go to school, but I knew this was not possible. I was willing to help my mother because I had a sense of togetherness. I felt as if the younger children were mine as well as my mother's. My whole salary went to the family. If there wasn't enough, I did without.

In garment factories, women and girls worked long hours for miserable wages. Many developed tuberculosis and other lung diseases in the dusty shops. Others suffered from exhaustion.

Factory bosses constantly prodded garment makers to work faster and produce more each hour. During the busy season, from December to May, the young women worked overtime, with no additional pay. Sixteen-year-old Sadie Frowne worked in a factory making skirts. She recalled,

Garment workers bent over their task sometimes for more than twelve hours a day.

At seven o'clock [in the morning] we all sit down to our machines and the boss brings to each one the pile of work that . . . she is to finish during the day, what they call in English their "stint." This pile is put down beside the machine and as soon as a skirt is done it is laid on the other side of the machine. Sometimes the work is not all finished by six o'clock [at night] and then the one who is behind must work overtime.

The large number of factories in New York produced intense competition. Bosses looked for ways to reduce costs and increase profits. They saved money by keeping wages low. But no matter how low the pay, owners always had a constant supply of willing workers, as new immigrants continued to pour into the city looking for jobs. As one factory owner explained, "These greenhorns [newcomers], Italian people, Jewish people, all nationalities, they cannot speak English and they don't know where to go and they just come from the old country and I let them work hard, like the devil, and those I get for less wages."

As more and more women flocked to factories, conditions worsened. Eventually, workers sought to improve their lot. They could do this, they reasoned, by joining together and forming unions.

CHAPTER 2

GATHERING
STORM

"It was a world of greed;
the human being didn't
mean anything."

—Pauline Newman, factory worker, n.d.

The surge of urban and industrial growth at the turn of the twentieth century brought with it a host of social problems. In large cities, tenements were overcrowded and disease ridden. Alcoholism, crime, and prostitution increased. Workers toiled in unsafe and unhealthy conditions.

Reform-minded Americans wanted to remedy such ills. They hoped to eliminate urban problems and close the gap between rich and poor. Some reformers sought to outlaw the sale of alcohol, which they believed led to other social ills. Others worked to fight corruption in government and to regulate unfair business practices. Many also wanted to outlaw child labor, improve working conditions in factories, and improve living conditions in urban slums.

Reformers in New York City made advances in the areas of housing and public health. City lawmakers passed new building codes to prevent overcrowding in tenements. The city also improved sanitary services, including garbage, sewer, and water systems.

Reforming labor laws was more difficult, however. To protect their profits, employers often fought against labor reform. When workers went on strike, employers hired strikebreakers, or replacement workers. Employers sometimes hired private detectives to harass strikers and protect strikebreakers, while the police often arrested striking workers. Strikes sometimes turned violent, with clashes between strikers and strikebreakers, private detectives, and police. But workers continued to strike. During the late nineteenth and early twentieth century, coal miners, bricklayers, carpenters, and other workers all demanded higher wages, shorter workdays, and better working conditions.

LIFE IN A SHIRTWAIST FACTORY

New York's garment factories produced most of the nation's men's clothing and three-quarters of all women's clothing. Shirtwaist makers were 85 percent female, 75 percent between the ages of sixteen and twenty-five. The working hours varied from shop to shop, but shirtwaist makers typically worked fifty-six, fifty-eight,

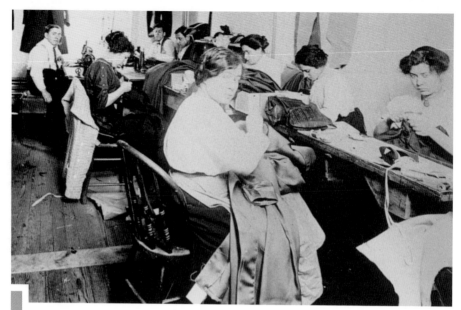
Garment factories in the early 1900s were usually dirty, crowded, and unsafe.

or sixty hours a week. The work was seasonal, which meant extra hours during the busy season and months of unemployment each year.

Pauline Newman began working at the Triangle Waist Company, one of the largest shirtwaist factories in the city, when she was eleven years old. She started work at seven-thirty in the morning and worked until nine in the evening. Many shirtwaist makers worked seven days a week. At the Triangle Waist Company, a sign in the elevator reminded workers: "If you don't come in on Sunday you need not come in on Monday!" Workers could be fired, fined, or sent home for the day for being late or missing work. "When a girl comes five minutes too late she is compelled to go home," said a Triangle worker. "[Her reason] does not matter, she must go home and loses a day."

Clara Lemlich became a shirtwaist maker shortly after her arrival in New York. "The bosses in the shops are hardly what you would call educated men," she said, "and the girls to them are part of the machines they are running. They yell at the girls and they 'call them down' even worse than I imagine the Negro slaves were in the South." Lemlich recalled, "The hissing of the machines, the yelling of the foreman made life unbearable."

The fictional "Gibson Girl" was the creation of illustrator Charles Dana Gibson. His drawings often appeared in popular magazines such as *Harper's*, *Collier's*, and *Scribner's*. The Gibson Girl was an attractive young woman—tall, graceful, high-spirited, and independent. Her clothes enhanced her charms. She wore a long-sleeved, high-collared shirtwaist that showed off her tiny waist. Her hair was usually knotted on top of her head, often adorned by a feather or hat. The Gibson Girl was the American ideal. She was refined, elegant, and stylish, and every young woman wanted to look like her.

The Gibson Girl image was so popular that the market for shirtwaists grew. Factories sprang up all over New York to meet the growing demand. By 1909 New York had more than five hundred shirtwaist factories employing approximately forty thousand workers.

Many models posed as Gibson girls, including Belgian-born actress Camille Clifford. She posed for this photo in 1900.

■ PROFITS FIRST—SAFETY LAST

A typical shirtwaist factory was crowded, with rows and rows of long tables covered with sewing machines. The roar and whir of the machines caused the floor to vibrate, but the young women bent over their work, their eyes intent on the flashing needles, tried not to notice. Workers pushed themselves so they would receive their full pay at the end of the week. The foreman constantly prodded the women to work faster. "The foreman is a bad driving man," said an eighteen-year-old named Rachael. "Ugh! He makes us work fast—especially the young beginners."

Workers had to be accurate too. According to Sadie Frowne,

Foremen *(background left, in vests)* look on as both male and female workers carry out their tasks at a garment factory.

"All the time we are working the boss walks about examining the finished garments and making us do them over again if they are not just right. So we have to be careful as well as swift."

In this era, few laws regulated safety in factories, and many shirtwaist shops were firetraps. Some bosses locked the doors, so that workers could not sneak out early or steal merchandise, but in the event of fire, workers would be trapped. Workrooms had no sprinkler systems, and some had no fire escapes. Others had rickety fire escapes that did not reach all the way to the ground.

■ ■ ■ ■ BORING AND REPETITIVE

Manufacturers broke down the process of making shirtwaists into simple steps that could be done by unskilled workers. All day some women sewed cuffs, others stitched sleeves, and others sewed on buttons. The work was monotonous. Women performed the same tasks over and over again, twelve to fourteen hours a day. The jobs that required more skill, such as cutting fabric, generally fell to men. They earned higher wages than the unskilled female laborers.

Factory workers were not allowed to talk during business hours, and owners placed women of different ethnic groups side by side to make communication difficult if women did try to talk. For instance, an Italian woman who spoke only Italian would be placed next to a Russian Jew who spoke only Yiddish. Bosses even limited trips to the restroom. According to Pauline Newman, "If you were two or three minutes longer than the foremen or foreladies thought you should be, it was deducted from your pay."

Male bosses often sexually harassed female workers. Those who repelled the unwanted advances might be threatened with dismissal. One young woman complained that the owner of the shop where she worked pinched workers' rear ends whenever they walked past. The young woman asked Rose Schneiderman, a union official, to speak to the boss about his behavior. When Schneiderman confronted the man, he replied, "Why, Miss Schneiderman, these girls are like my children." Schneiderman's response was quick and to the point: "We'd rather be orphans."

◾◾◾ THE SUBCONTRACTOR SYSTEM

Shirtwaist makers were paid several different ways. Some workers were paid a weekly salary, but most were paid by the piece—a certain amount for each item sewed. This arrangement compelled workers to produce as much as possible. "The faster you work the more money you get," recalled Sadie Frowne. "Sometimes in my haste I get my finger caught and the needle goes right through it. It goes so quick, tho, that it does not hurt much. I bind the finger up with a piece of cotton and go on working."

Another arrangement involved subcontractors. Under this system, a factory owner hired another employer, who in turn hired a team of workers. The factory owner assigned certain sewing machines in the shop to the subcontractor's employees. The owner paid the subcontractor a set price, for example, twenty-five dollars a week. The subcontractor

Both men and women worked in the garment trades. Women usually held the lowest-paying jobs.

took a cut of the money and divided the rest between the subcontracted employees. These workers earned less than those employed directly by the factory. Factory owners liked this system because it kept wages low and freed them from responsibility in case of accidents or injuries suffered by workers on the job.

Regardless of how they were paid, most shirtwaist makers earned barely enough to survive. The average wage was five dollars a week. But factory owners found ways to reduce this amount. Some bosses charged workers for the use of sewing machines, for the electricity to run the machines, for broken needles, and for ruined fabric. Workers were sometimes "taxed" for their chairs and for the lockers that held their hats. "Whenever we tear or damage any of the goods we sew on, or whenever it is found damaged after we are through with it, whether we have done it or not, we are charged for the piece and sometimes for a whole yard of the material," recalled Clara Lemlich.

Immigrant women accepted the poor working conditions in shirtwaist factories because they needed to work to survive. As one fifteen-year-old worker explained, "I make $3 a week. I have to help support the family. Father is out of work, and we have three younger children."

Factory jobs were often the only jobs available to such young women. And for every worker dismissed, employers knew there were dozens of women waiting to take her place. If a boss decided not to pay full wages, workers had no recourse, no way to make them do what was fair. When the busy season was over, workers were often laid off. Workers in this era received no welfare, no sick pay, and no unemployment insurance.

■ ■ ■ EARLY UNIONS FOR WOMEN

The American Federation of Labor, formed in 1886, was the most important trade union at this time. The AFL was devoted to protecting the interests of skilled workers. It organized workers into smaller unions according to their specific occupations. For instance, the AFL had unions for those who made cloaks (coats), shirts, cigars, boots and shoes, and for bookbinders.

Most AFL unions prohibited female members. Union leaders reasoned that female workers would marry and leave the workforce after a few years of labor and therefore did not need a union. In addition, many men did not think women should work outside the home at all.

But the situation began to change at the start of the twentieth century. In 1900 Samuel Gompers and other AFL leaders formed a union of all crafts in the women's garment trade. They called it the International Ladies Garment Workers Union (ILGWU). The ILGWU included smaller unions for cloak makers, skirt makers, tailors, and other workers. Union members were both male and female.

Samuel Gompers, shown here in 1914, helped organize the ILGWU.

Three years later, in 1903, a group of reform-minded women created the Women's Trade Union League. Membership was open to all women who supported trade unionism, whether they were members of a union or not. Women of wealth as well as working women joined the league, which dedicated itself to improving the general condition of female wage earners. League members fought to expand educational opportunities for working women, improve conditions in factories, and establish an eight-hour workday and a minimum wage for women. They also sought to end night work for women and to end child labor.

A TRIANGLE STRIKE

In 1906 New York shirtwaist workers founded their own union within the ILGWU. This union was called Local 25.

The word *ladies* in the name International Ladies Garment Workers Union refers to the type of garment produced, women's garments, not to the gender of the workers who sewed them.

Factory owners did not want their workers to join trade unions, but they pretended to be sympathetic to workers' interests. The Triangle Waist Company, for instance, created an "employees benevolent association," or company union. This organization was not a true trade union. It offered a few token concessions to workers, designed mainly to keep them quiet without cutting into business profits.

Triangle workers refused to join the company union. In September 1909, they met secretly to discuss joining Local 25. Apparently, the secret leaked out. A few days after the meeting, Triangle's owners locked the factory doors and laid off the workers. There was no work, the owners said.

The following day, Triangle advertised in the newspapers for new workers. The original workers saw the notices and realized the bosses had lied when they said there was no work. They also learned that the factory would not hire them back. So they joined Local 25 and declared a strike against Triangle. Shirtwaist makers at the Leiserson Shirtwaist Factory also went out on strike.

The strikers picketed in front of their factories, but the protests did not seem to accomplish anything. The owners found lots of unemployed workers to take the strikers' places. Talk of a general strike—a strike aimed at the shirtwaist industry as a whole—began to take hold. On November 22, 1909, the shirtwaist makers voted to launch a citywide strike. The massive walkout the following day was the beginning of a long and bitter struggle.

CHAPTER 3

THE UPRISING
OF TWENTY THOUSAND

"It is not riches or luxuries that they are fighting for—only a living wage, a little more freedom, the right to co-operate with each other for their common defense."

—Theresa Malkiel, labor activist in the shirtwaist strike, 1909

After the initial walkout on November 23, 1909, the striking shirtwaist makers marched to union headquarters, set up in a building called Clinton Hall. From shops all over the city, they surged into the seven-story building, filled every meeting room, jammed the hallways, and choked the stairways. Those who could not get into the building milled about outside, disrupting traffic and clogging the street. They came in greater numbers than anyone had anticipated. A mixture of English, Italian, and Yiddish rose and fell through the excited crowd. Jewish peddlers with trays suspended from their shoulders walked slowly through the crowd, selling pretzels and apples for a penny or two. A festive mood hung in the air—a feeling of confidence for a quick and easy victory.

Between twenty and thirty thousand workers—50 to 75 percent of the shirtwaist trade—answered the strike call. Most of the strikers and strike leaders were Jewish. Many of them were familiar with the ideals of Socialism and the labor movement. Italian women, by

The striking shirtwaist workers set up their headquarters at Clinton Hall in New York City. The building is shown here in the late 1890s.

contrast, were less active in the strike. They were used to obeying their husbands, fathers, and other authority figures. They were hesitant to defy their bosses and walk off the job. Like other shirtwaist workers, their families also desperately needed their income.

■ ■ ■ GETTING ORGANIZED

Running a strike takes a lot of work, and the shirtwaist makers needed to get organized. The WTUL stepped in and handled the job. It set up an information bureau on the ground floor of Clinton Hall, and WTUL leaders enrolled strikers in the union. Workers paid $0.10 to join. They paid the remaining dues of $1.25 in installments. League members also organized fund-raising events. They set aside money to pay a few dollars per week to needy strikers.

Striking workers and WTUL staff meet at Clinton Hall in 1909.

The league rented more than twenty meeting halls on the Lower East Side. It grouped the strikers by shop and placed a chairwoman in charge of each group. Esther Lobetkin, a Russian immigrant, was a typical chairwoman. All day long, she kept a close watch on her strikers and kept them informed of the latest developments. She also reported to headquarters and attended meetings until the wee hours of the morning. She typically grabbed a sandwich on the run, snatched a few hours of sleep, and then started all over again.

Each day, strikers held meetings at the various assembly rooms. There, union leaders urged workers to join the union and to persuade their fellow workers to join too. They encouraged the women to remain on strike and not give up. Meanwhile, ordinary workers shared stories from their factories and inspired the crowds. They traveled to different assembly rooms and spoke to enormous groups of striking workers who packed the halls to hear them. In one assembly room, a slight, pale nineteen-year-old striker stood onstage before her fellow strikers and urged, "Girls, from the bottom of my heart, I beg you not to go back to work. We are all poor, many of us are suffering hunger, none of us can afford to lose a day's wages. But only by fighting for our rights, and fighting all together, can we better our miseries; and so let us fight for them to the end!"

Reporters frequently visited union headquarters. The impromptu speakers impressed them. According to the *Call*, "Oratory seems to come naturally to these young women who speak Yiddish. . . . They can talk—oh, they can talk!—from the moment the master of ceremonies permits them to mount the stage until the urgency of another prompts the master to cut them off in their eloquence."

■ ■ ■ THE STRIKERS' DEMANDS

The striking workers developed a list of general demands for all shirtwaist factories. The most important demand was that shirtwaist factories would operate as closed shops. This meant that factory owners would hire only union workers.

Many striking shirtwaist workers dressed stylishly. They wore large hats festooned with feathers and flowers. Reporters often focused on the physical appearance of the young women and clouded the central issues—low pay and dangerous working conditions. Strike leaders defended the workers' right to dress fashionably. "We're human, all of us girls, and we're young. We like new hats as well as any other young women," wrote Clara Lemlich. "Why shouldn't we? And if one of us gets a new one, even if it hasn't cost more than 50 cents, that means that we have gone for weeks on two cent lunches—dry cake and nothing else."

Striking shirtwaist workers pose for a photograph in 1909.

Factory owners strongly objected to this demand. They felt they had the right to run their businesses as they saw fit, without interference from the union or anyone else. "All of this trouble," said Max Blanck, co-owner of Triangle Waist Company, "is over this union business. We did not recognize it, and we do not intend to. We told the girls that we were willing to listen to any complaints and to receive any suggestions from our employees themselves, but we had to draw the line on three or four east side gentlemen [union leaders] stepping in to tell us how to run our business."[36] Some factory bosses posted notices in their buildings that read, "This is an open shop. Employees will be engaged [hired] without regard to whether or not they belong to any labor organization."

Another general demand was an end to the subcontracting system with its extremely low wages. Workers also demanded a fifty-two-hour workweek with no more than two extra hours a day, weekly payment of wages, and an end to deductions from wages for materials and electricity.

Since each factory operated somewhat differently and conditions in one shop were not the same as conditions in another, union organizers also had to determine particular grievances and demands for each workplace. Strikers from each factory set up proposed wage scales, which outlined how much each worker would be paid, based on her job and years of experience. Strikers from each shop also decided on a proposed number of days off and paid holidays each year.

Meanwhile, union leaders began to negotiate with individual factory owners. Many small shirtwaist factories settled with the ILGWU the first week of the strike. They could not afford to remain idle. Once a settlement was reached, workers from that shop returned to the job.

PICKET DUTY

Some of the most important tasks were keeping striking workers on strike and getting nonstriking workers to join them. This work was done through peaceful picketing, a constitutional right of all Americans. On the second floor of Clinton Hall, union volunteers organized picket

Picketers used signs and banners to publicize their cause.

gangs "to see that none of the strikers scabbed." *Scab* is slang for a strikebreaker.

Factory bosses would not allow union members into their shops to talk to strikebreakers about joining the union. So strikers walked back and forth in front of the factories and urged working women to join the strike. They marched in shifts, a few hours in the morning when the factories opened and the strikebreakers were going to work and a few hours in the evening when the shops closed and the strikebreakers were leaving.

The Women's Trade Union League created a list of rules for picketers (also called pickets). The rules explained how striking workers should behave while on picket duty:

- Don't walk in groups of more than two or three.
- Don't stand in front of the shop; walk up and down the block.
- Don't stop the person you wish to talk to; walk alongside of him.
- Don't get excited and shout when you are talking.
- Don't put your hand on the person you are speaking to. Don't touch his sleeve or button. This may be construed as a "technical assault."
- Don't call anyone "scab" or use abusive language of any kind.
- Plead, persuade, appeal, but do not threaten.
- If a policeman arrests you and you are sure that you have committed no offense, take down his number and give it to your Union officers.

Picketing was also meant to bring work in the factories to a stop. If the strikers could convince enough workers to join them, factories would not be able to operate. Bosses would have to give in to worker demands or face financial ruin. Picketing also brought the poor working conditions in shirtwaist shops into the public eye.

But in 1909, many people saw picketing as improper behavior for women. Some thought it was unseemly for women to parade themselves on the street in public view. The picketing shirtwaist strikers challenged the stereotype of proper ladylike behavior. They also displayed strength, courage, and stamina—qualities that many associated with men rather than women. WTUL member Helen Marot explained:

> Picketing is a physical and nervous strain under the best conditions, but it is the spirit of martyrdom [sacrifice] that sends young girls of their own volition [will], often insufficiently clad and fed, to patrol the streets in mid-winter with the temperature low and with snow on the ground, some days freezing and some days melting. After two or three hours of such exposure, often ill from cold, they returned to headquarters, which were held for the majority in rooms dark and unheated, to await further orders.

■ ■ ■ THE PRESS JOINS THE FRAY

The shirtwaist makers strike became known as the Uprising of Twenty Thousand, or the Uprising of Girls, and newspapers printed daily reports on the strikers' struggles. Theresa Malkiel, a Russian Jewish immigrant and a staunch Socialist, wrote firsthand accounts of the strike for New York newspapers. In an article in the Socialist *Call*, she wrote:

> An uprising of women, a girls' strike! The average reader smiled as he read the first news of it. The average reader still thought that girls are flippy, flighty little things, working for pin money [extra spending money] and more interested in the style of hairdressing for the coming season than they would be in any organization, let alone a trade union. The average reader was doomed to disappointment. These "ignorant," "foreign" little girls had since shown a courage unsurpassed, a devotion to their cause unrecorded, a bravery to be admired.

Newspapers gave daily reports on strike statistics—which shops had settled and agreed to union demands, how many strikers were still out, and notices of meetings for strikers and their supporters. New York preachers even got in on the act. Many of them gave sermons supporting the strike. "These girls are not striking for automobiles or other luxuries," said Alexander Irvine at the Church of the Ascension. "They want only to earn enough to live, and every preacher and every paper should be with them."

■ EARLY VICTORIES

Union leaders set up a blackboard at strike headquarters to show which shops had signed union contracts. When a shop settled, it was noted on the board. Committee workers carried the news of factory settlements from hall to hall. Striking workers broke into storms of applause whenever they heard that an agreement had been reached.

The early settlements encouraged the workers still out on strike and gave them hope for a swift victory. According to a man named J. Goldstein, an ILGWU committee member, "The bosses are already signing up agreements, and several thousand of the strikers will return to work in the morning after gaining everything they demanded. Victory for all is sure!"

By Thanksgiving the strikers were elated. More and more shops had agreed to their demands. The *Call* reported that fifty-one factories had signed union contracts and more than seven thousand strikers were returning to work. Union and WTUL leaders believed the strike would end in a matter of days. Gertrude Barnum of the WTUL said, "This is the best Thanksgiving Day I have ever had. It is much better to see these poor girls winning their strike, and to assist them, than to eat turkey with cranberry sauce. I am glad to see the girls loyal, and I am pleased with the result of the struggle. I hope that it may speedily end in victory for all."

But the owners of the large shirtwaist factories were not so quick to settle. As Morris Hillquit, a union negotiator, explained to a group of strikers, "They [the factory bosses] like you, individually. They say to each of you that you are lovable, but when you, lovable girls, are formed into a bunch of lovable girls, then you cease to be lovable."

Factory owners banned together and fought back. They did all they could to keep the union out of their shops.

CHAPTER 4

FACTORIES
FIGHT
BACK

Starve to win, or you'll
starve anyway."

—Rose Pastor Stokes, writer and labor activist, 1909

As strikers presented their case to the public and press, factory owners also organized. On November 24, 1909, owners from approximately twenty large shirtwaist factories held a secret meeting to discuss ways to break the strike. They formed an organization called the Association of Waist and Dress Manufacturers of New York. Its goal was to crush the union. Association members vowed to fight the strike and to hire nonunion shirtwaist makers. The members unanimously passed a resolution supporting the open shop.

Manufacturers who had already settled with the union could join the association, provided they canceled their contracts with the union. Over the next several days, approximately one hundred shops signed a "no surrender" agreement with the association. Members vowed to break the strike by any means necessary.

To counter union arguments, the manufacturers association put out its own side of the story. It downplayed poor conditions in shirtwaist factories. A representative of the Bijou Waist Company said, "We cannot understand how so many people can be swayed to join in a strike that has no merit. Our employees were perfectly satisfied, and they made no demands. It is a foolish, hysterical strike, and not 5 per cent of the strikers know what they are striking for."

According to association president I. B. Hyman, "The strike leaders have been describing conditions which do not exist. They have represented the wages as about one-half, or less than one-half, what they really are, and unfortunately many people will believe these statements."

Hyman's argument itself was misleading. The wages of subcontract workers, the lowest paid of all shirtwaist makers, were not documented in company records. Hyman's claims were based on the wages of only regular employees and therefore did not give a true picture of wages for all shirtwaist workers.

THUGS AND PROSTITUTES

Factory owners resorted to even more sordid practices. They hired down-on-their-luck gangsters and hoodlums, in theory to "protect their property." In reality, the men were hired to beat up pickets and scare them out of striking. Breaking up strikes brought thugs quick and easy cash. Employers also hired prostitutes to harass the pickets. This was an effort to humiliate the strikers and to call their virtue into question. It sent the message that the strikers were no better than streetwalkers.

Newspapers filled with stories of clashes between pickets, strikebreakers, prostitutes, and "property protectors." On November 27, the *New York Times* reported, "A crowd of onlookers, which blocked all traffic, watched the combatants [strikers and prostitutes] while dresses were torn, faces scratched and the headgear of many girls on both sides were wrecked."

When the police arrived at skirmishes, brandishing batons, they usually arrested the pickets for disturbing the peace and let the thugs and prostitutes stroll away. According to a young woman picketing in front of the Triangle factory, "They hired immoral girls to attack us and they would approach us only to give the policemen the excuse to arrest us. In two weeks eighty-nine arrests were made. I, too, was arrested, and the policeman grabbed me by the hand and said such insulting words that I am ashamed to tell you."

Mary Dreier of the WTUL often joined the strikers on the picket lines. Day after day, she explained to the police that peaceful picketing was within the law and that the pickets wanted only to talk to the strikebreakers. But in many cases, factory owners had bribed police officers, so the arrests did not stop. "Whenever we spoke to the girls

Mary Dreier was president of the New York WTUL from 1906 to 1914.

[strikebreakers] the police would come up and gruffly order us to stop talking, and when we asserted our legal rights in the matter, persisted in their refusal to allow us to talk," said Dreier.

■ ■ ■ INTO COURT

The WTUL organized a volunteer legal staff to aid the arrested strikers. One group of volunteers raised bail, or money to get the arrestees released from police custody. Others appeared in court with the strikers.

In most cases, magistrates (similar to judges) sided with the police and factory owners. They fined strikers for disorderly conduct and disturbing the peace. After seeing dozens of strikers in his court night after night, Magistrate Krotel in the Essex Market Court told a striker, "You girls are getting to be a nuisance and menace to the community. I am here to do all in my power to stop this disorder." A judge named Olmsted lost his temper and shouted at another arrested striker, "God says in the Bible that by the sweat of his brow every man must earn his bread. You are keeping the girls [strikebreakers] from earning their bread. Your strike is a strike against God!"

Jennie Bloom was arrested while picketing in front of the Kaplan Waist Company and taken before a magistrate named Corrigan. He fined her ten dollars for disorderly conduct. He also told Bloom, "If any more strikers are brought before me I'll send them to the workhouse [a jail for people convicted of minor crimes]!" Indeed, some arrested strikers were sentenced to the workhouse. Others spent the night in jail cells with prostitutes, drunks, and criminals.

■ ■ ■ ROSE'S STORY

Fifteen-year-old Rose Perr shared her experience as a striker on picket duty with writers Sue Ainslie Clark and Edith Wyatt of *McClure's* magazine. Rose was tiny—most people guessed her to be twelve years old at most—and she wore her dark hair in braids. One morning as Rose and her friend Annie Albert were picketing in front of their factory, they approached a strikebreaker on her way to work. They intended to tell the worker about the strike and urge her to join them. The strikebreaker's male escort punched Annie. She fell to the ground, gasping for breath. Rose yelled for a police officer to help them. But when an officer arrived, he promptly arrested the two girls.

The police hauled the girls to the city jail. "They made me go into a cell," said Rose, "and suddenly they locked us in. Then I was frightened, and I said to the policeman there, 'Why do you do this? I have done nothing at all. The man struck my friend. I must send for somebody.' He said, 'You cannot send for any one at all. You are a prisoner.' We cried then. We were frightened. We did not know what to do."

Violet Pike bailed the girls out with WTUL funds and went with them to magistrate's court for their trials. A judge named Cornell sentenced the strikers to the workhouse. "I find the girls guilty," he said. "It would be perfectly futile for me to fine them. Some charitable women would pay their fines. . . . I am going to commit them to the workhouse under the Cumulative Sentence Act, and there they will have an opportunity of thinking over what they have done."

Rose Schneiderman and Mary Dreier went to see Judge Cornell about Rose's sentence. They explained to the judge that the strikers had done nothing wrong and that picketing was legal in New York. They tried to make him understand what it would mean to a young, impressionable girl to be locked up with thieves and drug addicts. "Oh," the judge responded, "it will be good for her. It will be a vacation."

Rose described her night in a downtown jail called the Tombs:

We walked to our cells. It was night, and it was dark—oh, so dark in there it was dreadful! There were three other women in the cell—some of them were horrid women that came off the street. The beds were one over the other, like on the boats [immigrant ships]—iron beds, with a quilt and a blanket. But it was so cold you had to put both over you; and the iron springs underneath were bare, and they were dreadful to lie on. There was no air; you could hardly breathe. The horrid women laughed and screamed and said terrible words.

Magistrates sent some striking workers to prison on Blackwells Island, shown here in 1933.

The next morning, Rose and Annie were taken by boat to a prison on Blackwells Island, in New York's East River. Upon arrival, they were stripped of their clothes and given dresses of coarse, heavy material. Rose's uniform was much too large for her. It trailed over her hands and dragged on the ground. A prison matron pinned it up with safety pins so that Rose could carry out her sentence of five days of hard labor—scrubbing floors and sewing gloves.

When their sentences were over, Rose and Annie left the island. A WTUL delegation greeted them when they got off the boat. Then the WTUL and the woman's committee of the Socialist Party held a reception and dance to honor Rose, Annie, and other strikers who had served time in the workhouse. WTUL member Leonora O'Reilly presented each young woman with a bouquet of American Beauty roses. "Usually a term in prison is looked on as a sign of degradation," said O'Reilly. But "there are cases in history where it has been a mark

At a meeting at Carnegie Hall, those strikers who had been sent to the workhouse sat near the front of the stage as a sign of honor. Other arrested strikers sat behind them.

of honor. These girls did no wrong, they violated no law. They were on duty for a cause, and bore their unjust imprisonment with fortitude. In their case imprisonment was an honor and not a degradation."

As the strike stretched on, week after grueling week, the strikers began to fight back. Even though the union told them over and over again to hold their tempers, some pickets got carried away in the heat of the moment. They called the strikebreakers scabs and sometimes resorted to violence. They tore strikebreakers' clothing and threw rotten eggs at them, employers, and the police. The police continued to haul the pickets off to jail. They arrested more than seven hundred shirtwaist makers during the strike.

■ ■ ■ SYMPATHY FOR THE STRIKERS

Sometimes middle- and upper-class women from the WTUL picketed with the workers. When these women were arrested, it brought added publicity to the strike. Once WTUL president Mary Dreier was arrested with a group of strikers. Dreier came from a prominent family and worked for the WTUL because she wanted to do something meaningful with her life. When the police officer who hauled Dreier into court learned who she was, he apologized for arresting her. "Why didn't you tell me you was a rich lady?" he asked. "I'd never have arrested you in the world."

League members made sure the press heard about the police bias in favor of the rich. They also used every opportunity to remind the press that there was no law against picketing and that pickets were simply exercising their constitutional right to express their opinions.

Newspapers wrote daily stories, complete with illustrations, of burly police officers and thugs shoving tiny teenage girls around. It was a bitterly cold winter, with more than the average amount of snow and freezing temperatures. Readers devoured stories of shivering young women in thin clothing, most of them without the luxury of a coat, as they walked back and forth in front of their shops to keep the strikebreakers away. "It takes uncommon courage to endure such physical exposure," said Helen Marot, "but these striking girls underwent as well the nervous strain of imminent arrest, the harsh treatment of the police, insults, threats and even actual assaults from the rough men who stood around the factory doors."

Public sympathy for the strikers grew, not only in New York but also in Philadelphia, Pennsylvania, Chicago, Illinois, and other cities with large numbers of women in the labor force.

■ ■ ■ NEW TACTICS BY THE OWNERS

The picketing had an effect on the Italian strikebreakers. Some of them became union members and joined the strike. But manufacturers found new ways to keep the others working. The Italians were mostly Catholics, so factory owners had Catholic priests talk to the strikebreakers. The priests told the workers that their duty as women was to be obedient and submissive. Some of the priests even told the workers that they would go to hell if they joined the strike.

Owners also used perks to entice strikebreakers to remain on the job. Triangle owners Max Blanck and Isaac Harris installed a crank-operated phonograph on the ninth floor of their factory and invited workers to dance on their lunch breaks. The bosses gave prizes to the best dancers. Owners also gave strikebreakers special food and drove some workers to and from the job in automobiles, a luxury few shirtwaist makers had ever experienced.

It was the start of the busy season. Manufacturers were desperate to keep their shops running at full capacity to meet their orders. To fill open jobs, factory owners recruited African American women to work as strikebreakers. Normally, black women were rare in shirtwaist and other factories. Many employers of this era would not hire African Americans. Most unions would not admit them as members.

A fierce debate sprang up in the African American community about whether black women should work as strikebreakers. Some women took the jobs as a way to break into the garment industry. Others joined the strikers, because they felt their best chance at true equality was through the union. They used their energies to pressure the ILGWU to admit them as members (which it soon did).

> "It takes uncommon courage to endure such physical exposure. But these striking girls underwent as well the nervous strain of imminent arrest, the harsh treatment of the police, insults, threats and even actual assaults from the rough men who stood around the factory doors."
>
> —Helen Marot, December 1910

Max Blanck *(left)* **and Isaac Harris** *(right)* **owned the Triangle Waist Company in New York City.**

The shirtwaist makers and their strike captured the nation's attention. Years later, a female labor leader wrote "Hail the Waistmakers of 1909," a tribute to their courage and determination:

In the black of the winter of nineteen nine,
When we froze and bled on the picket line,
We showed the world that women could fight
And we rose and won with women's might.

Hail the waistmakers of nineteen nine,
Making their stand on the picket line,
Breaking the power of those who reign,
Pointing the way, smashing the chain.

A MARCH TO CITY HALL

On December 3, 1909, more than ten thousand shirtwaist strikers held a massive parade. The striking workers rode in automobiles covered with signs or marched with banners. The messages read, "Fifty-two hours a week," "Peaceful picketing is the right of every woman," and "The police are for our protection, not for our abuse."

Striking shirtwaist workers in New York marched in a parade in December 1909. One carried a sign that read, "The police are for our protection, not our abuse."

A delegation from Local 25 and the WTUL broke off from the main parade route and marched to city hall. They wanted to publicly protest the harsh treatment of strikers by police, present a written protest to Mayor George McClellan, and ask him to investigate. A committee of

During the December 3, 1909, picket parade, some of the striking workers broke off and marched to city hall in New York City to talk to the mayor.

three WTUL members and three strikers who had been arrested waited for the mayor to return from lunch. When he did, they presented him with their official protest:

> We, the members of the Ladies' Waistmakers' Union, a body of 30,000 workers, appeal to you to put an immediate stop to the insults, intimidations, and to the abuses to which the police have subjected us while we have been peacefully picketing, which is our lawful right.

We protest to you against the flagrant discrimination of the Police Department in favor of the employers, who are using every method to incite to violence.

The mayor promised to look into the matter and discuss it with Police Commissioner William Baker. Whether he did or not cannot be definitively proven, but police behavior did not change and the violence continued.

CHAPTER 5

SUFFRAGISTS
JOIN THE
FIGHT

"I think that I was born a suffragist, but if I hadn't been I am sure that the conditions of the working girls in New York . . . would have made me one."

—Rose Schneiderman, n.d.

At the height of the shirtwaist strike, the woman suffrage (voting rights) movement was in full swing. In 1909 only a handful of states permitted women to vote. New York was not one of them. Many women in New York and across the country were committed to gaining suffrage.

Strike leader Rose Schneiderman was also a dynamic leader of the New York Woman Suffrage Party. She spoke at both suffrage and labor events. She and other suffragists saw woman suffrage and the fight of striking shirtwaist workers as intertwined. The ballot would be "a tool in the hands of working women with which, through legislation, they could correct the terrible conditions existing in industry" she explained.

Rose Schneiderman speaks at a WTUL meeting in New York City in the early 1900s. She was a strong supporter of women's voting rights.

In 1869 the territory of Wyoming became the first U.S. locale to grant women the right to vote. In addition to voting in territorial elections, Wyoming women could also hold public office and serve on juries.

Schneiderman often told audiences that women needed the vote to make sure lawmakers did not ignore them. Professor Max Eastman, president of the Men's League for Woman Suffrage, agreed. "If women had the right to vote," he said, "there would be no such treatment of women as has come from the Magistrates in the shirtwaist strike."

The shirtwaist workers received the treatment they did, suffragists said, because they had no political power. Thus the cause of obtaining the vote and the cause of improving working conditions for women merged into one larger cause—a woman's cause. "It is no mere accident that in this fight the striking Jewish and Italian girls, the poorest of the poor, have the sympathy and active support of the suffrage workers of all classes," said union leader Morris Hillquit. "There is a certain common bond between women fighting for civil rights and women fighting for industrial justice."

Suffragists also saw the two issues as intertwined and believed that success in one would eventually lead to success in the other. "The industrial and women suffrage movement must go together in this strike," said Bertha Weyl, secretary of the strike committee. "In fact, as far as women are concerned, the two issues are inseparable. It is true that this strike is for higher wages and better conditions and has nothing to do with woman suffrage, yet the American Federation of Labor, with which the Shirtwaist Makers' Union is affiliated, stands committed to woman suffrage. We will probably win this strike in two weeks, while woman suffrage, which is the vital issue, may take from ten to fifty years to win."

While suffragists supported the strikers, they also worked to bring the striking factory workers over to their cause. Sophia Loebinger, editor of the *Suffragette*, toured the Lower East Side and spoke to groups of strikers. She stood on a makeshift platform, a chair placed on the sidewalk near picketing strikers, and explained how their causes were linked:

> I want you all to know that I sympathize with you in your struggle for a living wage and for decent conditions, and the suffragettes are going to help you gain what you are justly demanding.
>
> If your employers won't give you what you ought to have when you ask for it as women, for God's sake get up and fight for your rights as do men! What right have these men to refuse you an eight hour day? What right have they to employ children under 16 years of age and make them work nine hours a day?
>
> None of your strikes will ever amount to anything until you get the vote. How can you expect to get any proper legislation passed when the men [lawmakers] up at Albany [the New York State capital] are bribed by your employers? If you all had votes, however, things would be different.

■ STRIKERS DIVIDED

Striker leaders were divided on the issue of suffrage. Although many of them supported voting rights for women, they did not want to confuse the issue of workers' rights with suffrage. They wanted to keep the focus narrow, on their goal of unionizing workers and improving working conditions. Violet Pike explained the WTUL's position: "This is a strike, not a political movement, which the woman suffrage movement is. There may be suffragettes among the strikers, and I believe there are, but this is a trade union movement pure and simple."

In addition to the mixed feelings among strikers, suffragists also faced strong opposition from many prominent New Yorkers. Rose Schneiderman debated a New York state senator who opposed suffrage for women. "He was afraid that if women had the vote they would lose their feminine qualities," Schneiderman recalled. She then asked the senator, none too gently, which caused women to lose more of their beauty and charm: putting a ballot in a box or working long hours in factories under brutal conditions?

The Reverend Charles H. Parkhurst of the Madison Square Presbyterian Church ridiculed the idea of votes for women. He too said that voting was unladylike behavior. He cried from the pulpit, "We have the right to be indignant at any female . . . who will consent to stand before a crowd of womanly women and sow in their honest and eager hearts the seeds of sex antagonism. It is ungenerous, it bruises, it is ignoble [low]. Woman will get all she wants if she is woman in her way of getting it, but if she is man in her way of getting it she will not get more than half of what she wants."

ALVA BELMONT AND THE POLITICAL EQUALITY ASSOCIATION

Alva Smith Vanderbilt Belmont, a wealthy society matron, was a staunch supporter of woman suffrage and women's labor rights. She created and named herself president of the Political Equality Association, one of the city's most active suffrage organizations. Belmont also used her social position to support the shirtwaist strike. "The Political Equality Association recognizes the fact that women must organize politically as well as industrially," she said, "if they are to permanently secure the benefits of industrial freedom."

Belmont considered the strike a women's struggle rather than a labor issue. "It was my interest in women, in women everywhere

Alva Belmont, shown here in 1919, was a wealthy supporter of women's labor and voting rights. She created the Political Equality Association to fight for woman suffrage.

and of every class, that drew my attention and sympathies first to the striking shirtwaist girls," she said. "Women the world over need protection, and it is only through the united efforts of women that they will get it."

Alva Belmont worked tirelessly for women's rights and threw herself into the shirtwaist strike. She started a fund-raising campaign for the strikers. She donated one hundred dollars—a significant sum at the time—and appealed to New Yorkers to make similar donations. "In the name of humanity," said Belmont in the *New York Sun*, "these women must be assisted until they can get back the work through which they were enabled to live honestly if far from comfortably." Belmont also appeared on picket lines, organized meetings, and raised money to keep the strike going. She spoke to groups of women, both wealthy society women and striking factory workers, and used every opportunity to tie the shirtwaist struggle to woman suffrage. She even sent prosuffrage buttons to union headquarters.

Belmont made a splash wherever she went, and barely a week went by when she wasn't quoted in the New York newspapers. She enlarged the focus of the shirtwaist strike to include women's rights and democracy in general. Belmont told a group of high school girls that when she was their age, her dreams were limited by the constraints of her gender.

I never thought about doing anything for humanity myself or of writing any books or painting pictures or making myself famous in any way. All I wanted in my most ambitious moments was to bask in the reflected glory won by my husband and sons. . . .

It is your duty to do all you can for your country. The time has come for us American women to be great ourselves, independently of our husbands. We must not sit quietly by as we used to do, waiting for some man to come along and marry

The shirtwaist strikers joined forces with suffragists. Alva Belmont *(at podium)* said that if women were allowed to vote, they could better bring about labor reforms.

us. Every woman must take upon herself the responsibility of citizenship.

Factory owners were not happy about Alva Belmont's involvement in the shirtwaist strike. They wished she would go home to her Madison Avenue mansion and stay out of it. According to Charles Dushkind, attorney for the manufacturers, "The strike would have been settled long ago, but for the support of fanatical women. The strikers have received the assistance of women of wealth and social prominence because it was thought that to do so would help the woman suffrage movement."

■ A HIPPODROME MEETING

Alva Belmont rented the Hippodrome Theatre on December 5, 1909, for a mass meeting to support the shirtwaist strike. Between seven and eight thousand people gathered there for the largest labor meeting in New York's history. The theater filled to overflowing, the street outside the building was jammed, and police turned hundreds away at the door. Belmont had invited leading city officials, but they all declined the invitation. Although the meeting was called to

Shirtwaist strikers and supporters crowded into the Hippodrome Theatre on December 5, 1909, for a giant protest rally.

THE WORLD'S **LARGEST THEATER**

Built in 1905, the Hippodrome Theatre in New York City was the largest and one of the most successful theaters in the world. Lit by 40,000 electric lights, the theater also had an extensive hydraulic (water movement) plant. The plant could pump 8,000 gallons (30,280 liters) of water per minute into a huge glass water tank below the stage. Theater operators could raise the tank to the stage for swimming and diving shows.

support the shirtwaist strike, Belmont invited suffragists as well as trade unionists to speak. Flags of blue with white letters adorned both sides of the room and carried the messages, "Votes for Women," "We demand equal pay for equal work," and "Give women the protection of the vote."

A military band played while the lively audience waited for the speakers to begin. Union leaders passed around collection baskets to raise money for the strikers. The chairman of the gathering, the Reverend John Howard Melish, called the meeting to order. He told the listeners that the meeting had been called "to protest against the use of the police power by any one class in the community against another, and also to inform the public what the girls were enduring and what they wanted."

Prominent labor leaders spoke to the crowd, whose enthusiasm was described by the *New York Sun* as a noise "like six batteries of field guns letting go all at once." The Reverend Dr. Anna Shaw, a Methodist minister, medical doctor, and suffragist, spoke passionately about women's rights, suffrage, and unions. She brought the issues of suffrage and trade unionism together and reminded the listeners that the causes were related:

The Reverend Dr. Anna Shaw spoke about women's suffrage and labor rights at the Hippodrome meeting in December 1909.

Our cause is your cause, and your cause is our cause. Personally, I believe in trade unions. You can't strike a blow with one finger or two fingers, but when you want to strike you put all your fingers together, clinch them hard, and then let drive. That's what the workers must do with themselves if they would be effective.

Men keep telling us we should go back to the home and do the work our grandmothers did. We can't; the men have taken that work out of the home, have put it in factories, and we must go out of the home to do it. The sun never shone upon a generation whose women loved the home more than the women of this generation. We don't go out to work because we like it. We don't accept half pay in competition with men because we don't care for money. We do those things because we have to."

Socialist Rose Pastor Stokes also spoke. "I believe the ballot is only the means to a great end," she said. "I believe it will do the working women of this country little good unless they use it to free themselves industrially. I bring you a message from the working men and women of the whole country: Workers, unite. You have nothing to lose but your chains and you have the whole world to gain."

Rose Pastor Stokes was one of many Socialist leaders involved in the shirtwaist strike. She was quoting Karl Marx (*below*) when she urged the workers to unite at the Hippodrome meeting. Marx, a nineteenth-century German philosopher, social scientist, and historian, believed that the working class would someday rise up in revolution. He believed workers would create a classless society, in which everyone shared wealth equally.

Marx's ideas led to the Socialist movement. By the turn of the twentieth century, this movement was particularly strong in Russia and other European nations. It was also strong in large U.S. cities such as New York and Chicago. Many newly arrived immigrants embraced Socialism as a means to achieve social justice and economic equality in their new homeland. Many believed that unionism was crucial to the Socialist cause, because strong unions would protect working-class laborers and help bring about equality in living standards.

But many Americans, including most business owners and politicians, feared Socialism. They worried that Socialist radicals wanted to overthrow the U.S. government. Many people wanted to see the movement stamped out in the United States.

> "I bring you a message from the working men and women of the whole country: Workers, unite. You have nothing to lose but your chains and you have the whole world to gain."
>
> —Rose Pastor Stokes, Socialist, using Marxist language to call striking workers to unite, December 5, 1909

LET'S ARBITRATE

The same day as the Hippodrome meeting, December 5, 1909, ILGWU leaders Marcus Marks and John Mitchell sent a letter to I. B. Hyman, president of the Association of Waist and Dress Manufacturers. The union leaders suggested forming a committee to arbitrate the strike, or decide on a settlement. The proposed arbitration board would be made up of two members representing the workers, two members representing the employers, and two impartial members to be chosen by the other four. The employers accepted the offer the following day.

The arbitration board met on December 10. The workers were determined to have shirtwaist factories operate as closed (union-only) shops, but the manufacturers refused to discuss the issue. President Hyman, on behalf of the factory owners, stated, "The manufacturers would under no circumstances unionize their shops, nor agree to employ only union help, or enter into union agreements. . . they were perfectly willing to have any complaint of employees or grievances investigated, considered, and settled by the Arbitration Committee, but. . . the question of a 'closed shop' was not open for consideration." The meeting ended, and the attempt to reach an agreement by arbitration collapsed.

A TOUGH DECISION

On December 13, union representatives held a meeting to update strikers on their progress. They reported that 286 firms had settled with the union and nearly fifteen thousand workers had returned to work after obtaining their demands. Yet the large manufacturers would not agree to a closed shop, and this issue was key. Without unionized workplaces, bosses would have no obligation to uphold their agreements. They could easily renege on their promises to workers. Any concessions gained through the strike would quickly be lost.

Some strikers were ready to forgo the closed shop and settle with the manufacturers. The strikers were suffering, not just from picketing in frigid temperatures and from police harassment but also from poverty. Some of them had been evicted from their apartments because they could not pay the rent. Others were hungry because they could not afford food. Some women who had returned to work in shops that had settled were depriving themselves of food to help those who were still out of work.

But union leaders encouraged the remaining strikers to continue the strike. Rose Schneiderman explained that if the strikers returned to work on the open-shop plan, they would be no better off than before. The strikers ultimately agreed. At the December 13 meeting, they voted to remain on strike. They wanted a closed shop and would continue to strike until the factory owners agreed to this all-important demand.

By December 14, Alva Belmont's strike fund had grown to $1,525 in donations. Belmont gave the money to the WTUL, which distributed it to the most destitute strikers for food and rent. Since thousands of women were still on strike and funds were so limited, no striker received more than $2 a week.

Union chair J. Goldstein was impressed by the stamina of the strikers and supported them in the press. "I have been in the labor movement for many years," he told a reporter for the *Call*, "but I have never seen more enthusiasm and determination among a lot of strikers. There is the strongest spirit of solidarity among them that I have ever seen."

CHAPTER 6

THE MINK BRIGADE

"We not only wanted labor laws and bread, we wanted roses, too."

—Rose Schneiderman, n.d.

Alva Belmont looked for new ways to help the striking shirtwaist makers. One day Belmont telephoned a night court judge, asking if she should send her lawyer to help defend strikers who had been arrested. The judge's reply shocked Belmont. "You had better save your time and money," said the judge, "they are nothing but little Jew girls, and their place is the workhouse."

After that, Belmont worked harder than ever for the cause. She enlisted the help of the "four hundred." These were the wives and daughters of four hundred of the wealthiest men in the world. The women were the cream of New York society. The press dubbed them the Mink Brigade for their expensive mink fur coats.

ALVA AND ANNE

Anne Morgan, daughter of millionaire financier J. Pierpont Morgan, joined the WTUL to show her support for the strike. "I have only known something of this strike for a short time," she told a reporter for the *New York Times*, "and I find other people to whose attention it has not been brought do not know anything about it. If we come to fully recognize these conditions we can't live our own lives without doing something to help [the strikers], bringing them at least the support of public opinion."

Wealthy women such as Anne Morgan *(right)* often wore furs. Those who were supporters of the strikers were called the Mink Brigade.

Alva Smith Vanderbilt Belmont (*below*) was the daughter of an Alabama plantation owner. She married railroad heir William K. Vanderbilt in 1875, had three children, and became one of the most prominent socialites of the Gilded Age. This period of history, 1878 to 1889, saw a tremendous growth in industry, which produced many great fortunes. (*Gilded* means "covered in gold.")

As a Vanderbilt, Alva lived like royalty. She designed and built three spectacular mansions: a chateau (mansion) on Fifth Avenue in New York City; Idle Hour on Long Island, New York; and the grandest mansion of all, Marble House in Newport, Rhode Island. Designed to look like the Palace of Versailles in France, Marble House had creamy Algerian and Italian marble on the walls, floors, staircases, and even the driveway. Exquisite art from Europe, French carpets, and glittering gold adorned the fifty-room "cottage," which was kept in order by a staff of twenty-five.

Alva divorced Vanderbilt in 1895, a scandalous move at the time. She married banker Oliver Hazard Perry Belmont the following year, and the couple designed and built a mansion on Madison Avenue. After Oliver Belmont died suddenly in 1908, Alva became an ardent suffragist and women's rights activist.

New York attorneys Miles Dawson
(*above*) and Morris Hillquit (*right*)
represented some of the striking
workers in court for free.

Alva Belmont and Anne Morgan met with ILGWU leaders, the
WTUL, and several lawyers to settle on a plan to give the striking
pickets legal aid. The planners noted that when strikers appeared in
court, they rarely had witnesses or skilled lawyers to speak on their
behalf. The factory owners, on the other hand, always provided lawyers
and plenty of witnesses for the prosecution. As a result, an impartial
trial was impossible. The proceedings were always stacked in favor of
the manufacturers.

Belmont and Morgan outlined a legal aid campaign with several
main strategies. Union officials described the plan as "both brilliant
and daring." First, prominent New York attorneys Morris Hillquit,
Meyer London, and Miles Dawson volunteered to represent the
arrested strikers for free. They would go to the three day courts and one
night court in Manhattan, as well as to the Brooklyn court, to defend
strikers. "We are most anxious to co-operate with the police and the

courts in making clear to the pickets just what are their rights," said Dawson. "Our efforts are directed only toward seeing that the girls get an equal show along with the employers of peacefully winning the strike."

Second, Belmont and Morgan recruited college students to act as "watchers" to make sure that events on the picket lines were reported fairly and accurately in court. The students came from New York's Barnard College, Vassar College, and Columbia University. The watchers were not involved in the strike in any way, so they would be considered impartial witnesses. "The testimony of unbiased, impartial observers like yourself will be most valuable in placing the real facts before the courts and the public," wrote the *Call* in advertising for watchers. "The moral effect of such observations could not fail to be in the direction of peace and order."

Watchers carefully observed the pickets and took note of their actions and the actions of police. When a picket was arrested, a watcher would testify about what had happened on the picket line and who had started the fracas.

Miles Dawson took charge of the legal bureau for the striking workers. He made sure the strikers' rights were fully protected. "The highest court says that pickets have a perfect right to walk up and down before a strike shop and say to the non-union girls: 'Please do not take our places; we are working to better our conditions, and you are taking the bread and butter out of our mouths. We want you to join us so that we can win and you will benefit yourself at the same time.' Yet for doing this very thing that the court allows, these girls are arrested and sent to jail. It isn't right," said Dawson.

ALVA BELMONT MAKES HERSELF HEARD IN COURT

Alva Belmont also appeared in court with arrested strikers, sometimes from the start of night court at nine o'clock to its end at three o'clock the next morning. She often brought her lawyer with her to represent the young women. On her way out of court one morning, she met a reporter for the *Call*. She told the reporter:

During the six hours spent in that police court I saw enough to convince me and all who were with me beyond the smallest doubt of the absolute necessity for woman's suffrage—for the direct influence of women over judges, jury and policemen over everything and everybody connected with the so-called course of justice.

Every woman who sits complacently amidst the comforts of her home, or who moves with perfect freedom and independence in her own protected social circle, and says "I have all the rights I want," should spend one night in the Jefferson Market Court. She would then know that there are other women who have no rights which man or law or society recognizes.

At another session in night court, Belmont grew indignant after watching a judge sentence striking shirtwaist makers. On her way out of the courthouse, a reporter asked her what she thought about the proceedings. An angry Belmont replied, "I don't think the public would care to hear what I would like to say about this court. I might have something to say to-morrow, but not to-night. If you will just wait till we get women judges and newspapers run by women things will be different."

Belmont and other wealthy society women often paid the bail and fines of arrested strikers. One night in court, Belmont appeared to bail out four arrested strikers. The total amount due was eight hundred dollars. Since she did not have that much cash with her, Belmont offered her mansion on Madison Avenue as collateral, or backing, for the debt. The judge did not recognize her and asked if her house was worth eight hundred dollars. "I think it is," replied Belmont. "It is valued at $400,000."

A MEETING AT THE COLONY CLUB

On December 15, 1909, Anne Morgan organized a meeting at the Colony Club, one of the most exclusive private clubs in New York, to

Normally, only extremely wealthy women entered New York City's private Colony Club. But on December 15, 1909, shirtwaist workers—invited by Anne Morgan—visited the club to talk about the strike.

raise money for the striking shirtwaist makers. WTUL president Mary Dreier brought ten young strikers to the meeting. The shabbily dressed strikers provided a sharp contrast to the wealthy society women, decked in jewels and furs. The society women sat on gold-colored

Founded in 1903, the Colony Club was the first social club in New York City started by women for women. Modeled after male social clubs, the Colony Club admitted only the cream of New York society. Members had to pay an initiation fee and annual dues.

chairs in the sumptuous gymnasium of the club to learn about the strike firsthand from the teenagers and young women who were at the heart of it.

First, Mary Dreier shared the history of the strike and told the society women that about seven thousand shirtwaist makers were still out of work. She called the strike a battle and urged the wealthy women to help the strikers by contributing money to the strike fund. Dreier then introduced the factory workers, who told about their experiences as shirtwaist makers and strikers.

"I take $3.50 a week," said one striker. "It is that keeps our family. Three other children go to school, and my mother can't see good out of her eyes. That's all I've got to say. I am 15 years old." A young Italian woman explained that she earned six dollars a week. "Yes, I get 4 cents a dozen for waists," she said. "A priest came to our shop and told us girls that if we struck we should go—excuse me, please, ladies—to hell."

The wives and daughters of New York's millionaires were moved by the strikers' stories. They passed around two hats for donations, adding thirteen hundred dollars to the strike fund. After the speeches and the collection, the strikers and the society women shared tea.

A PICKET PARADE

A week after the Colony Club meeting, Alva Belmont, Anne Morgan, and the WTUL organized a picket parade of automobiles. Belmont and Morgan rode at the front of the parade. They were joined by some of their wealthy friends, who supplied fifteen luxurious, chauffer-driven cars. The cars bore posters that read, "Thirty thousand shirtwaist makers have joined our ranks," "We want shorter hours and higher wages," and "The workhouse is no answer to the demands for justice." The lead car's sign read, "Votes for Women."

Society women and the WTUL organized this picket parade on December 21, 1909.

The parade traveled down Fifth Avenue and then to the garment district. It drove past every shirtwaist shop where strikebreakers were still at work. As always, the strikers wanted to make an impression on strikebreakers and convince them to join the union. Mary Dreier explained that the automobiles were "very helpful in covering a large amount of territory in a hurry, as is necessary when the strikebreakers are going to and from work at the same hour." All along the route, people lined the streets and cheered.

Belmont also organized a group of wealthy women to visit New York's department stores and appeal to them to carry only union-made shirtwaists. They urged leisure-class women to patronize only stores that carried merchandise made by union workers. "Now is the time for women in New York, Philadelphia, and in fact everywhere American shirtwaists are worn, to rise in their might and demonstrate that with them bargain-hunting can be subordinated to [put lower than] principle and that they have said goodbye to the products of the sweatshop. . . . Friends, let us stop talking about sisterhood, and MAKE SISTERHOOD A FACT!"

SOCIALISTS RESENT THE MINK BRIGADE

Some observers criticized the wealthy strike supporters. They thought the Mink Brigade was involved in the strike for personal reasons: for attention, for the suffrage cause, or merely to ease the boredom of everyday life. In a letter to the editor, Irving E. Doob wrote in the *New York Times*, "Women of wealth but of unknown mental capability, suffragettes of means but of unknown experience, and persons who would be despised as religious renegades [deserters] by the mass of strikers—all these bestow their sympathies one way or the other to gain votes for women or the fleeting joy of a press notice."

Socialist Emma Goldman was outspoken in her censure (condemnation) of the role of wealthy women in the strike. She noted that the women's actions were charitable but did nothing to remedy the underlying system that allowed business owners to exploit workers in the first place. "If the strike is won," said Goldman, "it will be not on its merits but because it was assisted by wealthy ladies. It is all very sentimental and fine and kind for the ladies of the Colony Club to come forward, but they can help the girls better as a class by getting off their backs [leaving them alone]. I have no personal feeling against Mrs. Belmont or Miss Morgan, but their contributions will not harmonize capital [business owners] and labor. They will harm the labor movement, which to be successful must be entirely independent."

Others welcomed the involvement of the Mink Brigade. The strikers desperately needed financial support, and the wealthy women provided the funds to keep the strike going. They also brought front-page publicity to the strike.

Emma Goldman was a leading U.S. Socialist. Eventually, the government deported her—or forced her to leave the United States—for her political activism.

FACTORY OWNERS FIGHT BAD PRESS

Newspapers relied heavily on advertising income from the garment industry. They didn't want to offend shirtwaist manufacturers, who might pull their advertisements in response to negative press. So papers often printed various perspectives on the strike and some stories with an antiunion bias. At the same time, the public loved sensational stories about the strike. Stories about millionaires helping poor factory workers sold newspapers. In the end, public opinion still sided with the strikers.

But the manufacturers also used the press to gain support for their side of the controversy. In interviews with reporters, they claimed that conditions inside their factories were healthful and safe and that the striking women had no valid complaints. The New York Times printed a letter from the Association of Waist and Dress Manufacturers to Anne Morgan, asking her to check out factory conditions for herself: "We hereby formally invite such an examination, and hold ourselves in readiness to facilitate in every way a thorough investigation. We are led to communicate with you because of the part you have publicly taken during this strike, in order that members of this association may be given a 'square deal' before the public, and in reliance upon your sense of fairness." Anne Morgan declined the invitation.

PHILADELPHIA JOINS THE STRIKE

On December 19, 1909, a delegation of New York strikers attended a meeting in Philadelphia, Pennsylvania. They went to encourage Philadelphia shirtwaist makers to go on strike with their New York sisters. The shirtwaist makers had learned that some New York shirtwaist manufacturers, unable to operate normally during the strike, were subcontracting with factories in Philadelphia. If the New York strikers could convince the Philadelphia shirtwaist makers to join the strike, factory owners would be hard-pressed to complete their spring orders in either city. Manufacturers, the workers hoped, would be forced to settle or lose their profits for the year.

Conditions in shirtwaist factories in Philadelphia were much the same as conditions in New York. After listening to the New York strikers, members of the Women's Shirtwaist and Garment Makers' Union of Philadelphia voted to strike. The next morning, December 20, more than seven thousand of twelve thousand Philadelphia shirtwaist makers walked off the job.

CHAPTER 7

COLLEGE WOMEN
JOIN THEIR SISTERS

What you are doing not only helps me and other women in the struggle for life, as we know it today, but it is going to help the cause of all women workers who are to come."

—Ida Tarbell, a journalist, addressing
striking shirtwaist makers, 1910

College women joined the strike in December 1909.
Students from the nation's top women's colleges—Vassar, Bryn Mawr, Smith, Barnard, and Wellesley—rallied to the cause of the striking shirtwaist makers. Passionate about helping their less fortunate sisters, they donated both their time and money. Recent college graduates also joined the fight. Female nurses, lawyers, charity workers, social workers, librarians, and teachers volunteered for all kinds of jobs. College women acted as watchers on the picket lines to make sure that arrested strikers received fair treatment in court. College women also spoke at meetings and raised money for the strike.

PICKET DUTY

College women walked arm in arm with the shirtwaist makers on the picket lines. They were arrested with the strikers too. Henrietta Mercy was a graduate of New York's Normal College and the secretary of the East Side Equal Rights League. She was also the private secretary for a

College women joined the striking workers on picket lines in December 1909.

woman of wealth. Mercy marched on the picket lines to show her support for the strike. She described how she and the strikers walked peacefully in pairs up and down the street in front of a shirtwaist factory. As was typical, they wanted to talk to the strikebreakers as they came out of work and convince them to join the strike. "As the girls [strikebreakers] got ready to come out of the factory, between twenty and thirty special policemen employed by the factory as guards for the workers, formed a double line on the sidewalk, one line on the curb line and the other along the building, or the Greene Street side," said Mercy. "They hurled themselves upon us and threw us off the sidewalk onto the pavement. They threw us so hard that some of the girls fell on the stones. We tried to get back on the sidewalk and they shoved, elbowed and even kicked some of us to keep us in the street."

Violet Pike was a Vassar graduate and a teacher in a private school. She stood in front of a shirtwaist factory, wearing a large cardboard sandwich sign (with one placard in front of her and one in back) with an appeal for help for the strikers. She spoke to a crowd that had gathered around to hear her. A police officer named Ahrens ordered Pike to move on. She refused and told him that as a citizen, she had a right to speak where she pleased. "All right," said Ahrens, "you can speak if you have a permit. If you haven't you will have to get one, move on, or be arrested." According to Ahrens, Pike replied, "I haven't a permit. I don't intend to get one, and I don't intend to stop speaking. Go ahead and arrest me if you dare."

The police officer dared. He arrested Pike, took her to the Jefferson Market Police Court, and threw her into what she described as a "filthy pen." Nine and a half hours later, at two thirty the next morning, Pike appeared before the judge. The judge did not think she had committed a crime, and she was discharged. Pike had this to say about her experience:

> My arrest and imprisonment was an outrage, and somebody will be made to suffer for it. I am interested in the cause of the girl strikers because I believe that they have been unjustly and cruelly treated by their employers, and I admire them for the brave and courageous stand they have taken in endeavoring to better their condition in life.

Just as American women had to fight for their rights in the workplace, women also had to fight for the right to be educated. In earlier centuries, American society considered women to be mentally inferior to men and unsuited to higher education. Some people argued that women could not stand the physical strain of college study. They said that women were frail and that too much study would give them "brain fever" and even impair their ability to have children. Some argued that higher education for women was pointless, since they were supposed to get married and have children, not work outside the home.

Some educators did support higher education for women, but they proposed separate women's colleges, so that women would not "pull down" the quality of education at all-male universities. In the late nineteenth century, educators founded several women's colleges in the northeastern United States.

Early college women came from well-to-do families. Their college curriculums focused primarily on preparing them to be good wives and mothers, secondarily on preparing them for suitable "woman's work," such as teaching. A 1910 article about college women in the *New York Times* illustrates prevailing attitudes at the time: "In every case wherein the young woman is successfully prepared for the duties of making a happy home for a worthy husband and noble children the [human] race is thereby lifted one notch higher toward God."

The *New York Times* described Elsie Cole, another Vassar graduate, as a skilled and eloquent speaker. Arrested three times while picketing, she "pleaded her case so effectively that the policemen on duty have no mind to interfere with her again. Even the bosses know her and are afraid of her. They call her 'that woman that talks' because she can make a full-fledged argument and win her point while the boss is struggling for the words to form a single sentence."

The strikebreakers did not appreciate the addition of college women to the ranks of pickets they had to face each day. Like all shirtwaist workers, the strikebreakers were poor and worked to support their families, but they did not believe they could survive if they gave up their wages to join the strike. "We want women to stand together and fight for each other," one college picket told a strikebreaker, "because you know you can do nothing alone."

"It's all very well for you to say that," replied the strikebreaker. "You are well dressed and well fed. You have money enough to live on, you don't have to work. What do you know about my position?" Factory bosses also had harsh words for the college women. One manufacturer told a college student, "You women that ain't got anything to do think it's stylish to butt in."

First Daughter Helen Taft promised to tell her father, President William Howard Taft, about the plight of striking workers.

■ ■ ■ PICKETING IN PHILLY

Helen Taft, daughter of President William Howard Taft, visited Philadelphia and became interested in the shirtwaist strike there. "I certainly sympathize with the poor little girls," she said. "I never knew they were so downtrodden. Really, I'll never put on a shirtwaist again without a shudder. . . . I certainly shall speak to papa about the terrible conditions under which these poor girls are compelled to live."

Smith College graduate Martha Gruening also traveled to Pennsylvania. She picketed with the Philadelphia strikers, was arrested, and spent a night in jail. "I was treated as if I had already been convicted of some crime instead of being before the law," she said. She described the jail as disgusting, so dirty that she was afraid to sit down. "It is like going back into the Dark Ages."

The next morning, Gruening went before Magistrate Scott for her hearing. "It is women like you who have caused all this trouble, and not the actual strikers," said the judge. "Had you and your kind kept your hands off, it would have been over long ago." Gruening was sentenced to Moyamensing Prison.

The presence of college women on the picket lines and the publicity generated by their arrests had an immediate effect. The police had been arresting and hauling poor factory workers off to jail for weeks. But when wealthy college women received the same

"I was treated as if I had already been convicted of some crime instead of being before the law," she said. She described the jail as disgusting, so dirty that she was afraid to sit down. "It is like going back into the Dark Ages."

—Martha Gruening, on being arrested while picketing with striking shirtwaist workers in Philadelphia, Pennsylvania, January 1910

treatment and stories of their arrests appeared in newspapers, the people of New York and Philadelphia took notice. The number of arrests decreased.

In late December, Rabbi Goldstein, the chaplain (religious counselor) of the New York jail the Tombs, met with Magistrate Cornell. Cornell had sentenced many strikers, including Rose Perr, to the workhouse. The rabbi convinced the judge that sending young women from respectable families to the workhouse was wrong. It exposed them to "moral contamination," Goldstein said. Decent women, explained the rabbi, would have to associate with prostitutes and criminals behind bars. Judge Cornell reversed his previous practice and began to fine the strikers and place them on probation.

■ ■ ■ ■ WINTER HARDSHIPS

As New Yorkers prepared for the holiday season, the strikers' spirits sagged as low as the freezing temperature. Jewish strikers celebrated Hanukkah. Italians celebrated Christmas. But none of the strikers had money to buy gifts for their loved ones. Many of them did not even have money to buy food. "In this charitable city every homeless man may have turkey on Christmas Day," said Eva McDonald Valesh of the committee to aid the strikers, "but there will be no turkey to-morrow for most of the striking shirtwaist makers. There is no charitable organization to provide a Christmas meal for poor [striking] women."

The worst snowstorm in twenty years hit New York City on Christmas Day 1909. A bitter cold snap followed the storm, and knifing winds cut through the narrow streets of the Lower East Side. Some strikers left the picket lines for the hospital to be treated for frostbite. "There never was anything like it!" said a male union organizer. "An equal number of men never would hold together under what these girls are enduring."

The WTUL appealed to grocery stores for donations of tea, coffee, sugar, and sandwiches for the hungry strikers. It set up a lunch wagon

Striking shirtwaist workers picketed throughout the cold, snowy Christmas season of 1909.

with coffee and sandwiches in the garment district so that pickets could eat without leaving their places on the picket line. As the strike wore on, the atmosphere at union headquarters in Clinton Hall changed from "five floors full of gayety and laughter to five floors full of sighs and sad eyes."

IN SEARCH OF FUNDS

By the end of the year, funds were low and many of the striking workers were getting desperate. The majority of them had families to support, and more than a month without wages had taken its toll. Union leaders did not want to let hunger and discouragement force the workers back to their jobs. Union leaders thought the strikers could win if they could hold out long enough.

The WTUL printed postcards asking for donations and sent them to wealthy citizens of New York. Newspapers such as the *Call* printed passionate appeals.

THESE GIRLS NEED HELP. They need money for food, for rent, for clothes, for the necessities of life. Winter at its worst is now upon us and these things must be had. That money must come from YOU—YOU who read this—YOU who sympathize with these brave girls fighting for the chance to work honestly and to live decently—YOU who want to see them win because they deserve to win. . . . EVERY DOLLAR WILL COUNT IN THIS FIGHT FOR FREEDOM, FOR WOMANHOOD, FOR JUSTICE, AND AGAINST TYRANNY, DEGRADATION AND INJUSTICE.

In response, New Yorkers gave money in large and small amounts. In addition to cash, some wealthy women donated gold chains, earrings, and lockets.

■ ■ ■ EXTRA! EXTRA! READ ALL ABOUT IT!

The *Call* printed a special edition, devoted entirely to the story of the strike, to raise money for the strikers. The paper told the history of the strike from the viewpoint of the strikers themselves. It included articles about the treatment of strikers by police and judges, a list of manufacturers that had settled with the union, and an appeal for financial support. Some articles were in Yiddish and Italian. The paper also included a number of poems and cartoons.

The special issue was not sold on newsstands. Instead, wearing banners that read "Ladies' Waist Makers' Union on Strike for Better Conditions," striking workers and college students sold the paper on city streets. They fanned out across the city to sell the newspaper on Wall Street, in Washington Heights, and at Columbia University. They stood in front of Madison Square Garden, Macy's department store, the Hotel Astor, and the Waldorf Astoria. They sold papers to professors and students, and laborers and financiers. One elderly woman paid five dollars for a paper that normally sold for five cents. A rich gentleman on Broadway donated ten dollars for a copy of the paper.

At the Brooklyn Bridge, a striker selling papers met a woman coming out of the subway. The woman had heard that manufacturers were threatening to stop making shirtwaists altogether—to shut down their businesses as a way to punish the strikers. "There's a lot of women who would rather be shirtless than heartless," the woman told the striker as she bought a newspaper. "I hope you'll win your strike!" By two in the afternoon, the paper had sold out, and the *Call* printed another edition. The strikers sold tens of thousands of copies.

Even though it was cold and most of the strikers did not have gloves or warm coats, they were happy to earn money for their

Shirtwaist strikers sell a special edition of the *Call* to raise money for the strike fund. A sign in Yiddish, not uncommon on the heavily Jewish Lower East Side, hangs behind them.

cause. "Isn't this fine?" asked a young woman in front of Macy's. "I've got more than twice the price for every paper sold. Some of us girls who were going to be put out of our rooms for owing rent will be fixed all right now. It seems good to be earning money. The wealthy women have helped us, but we like to be able to do something for ourselves."

■ ■ ■ ■ A VOTE ON SETTLEMENT

Shirtwaist factory owners were feeling the effects of the strike. Their profits for the year were in jeopardy, and they needed to complete their spring orders. Each week a few more shops settled with the union and agreed to sign contracts. In late December, ILGWU officers and representatives for the manufacturers met to discuss a settlement plan for the six thousand strikers still out of work. The negotiators reached a tentative agreement, and both sides planned to meet with their respective groups to vote on the proposal.

The proposed agreement provided for a fifty-two-hour workweek, with no more than two hours extra work per day. Employers agreed to furnish, free of charge, needles, thread, and all other supplies needed for making shirtwaists. They agreed to offer four paid holidays each year. They also agreed to give the striking workers their jobs back. They would not, however, agree to hire only union workers. "We insist upon an open shop," said I. B. Hyman, "the right to employ union and non-union employees without discrimination, and from that stand we will not budge."

On December 27, 1909, the strikers met at five large meeting halls on the Lower East Side to vote on the proposal. Only union members were allowed to attend the meetings, with workers grouped by shop. At Beethoven Hall, a union official read the proposal before the packed crowd. When he reached the section that stated that factories would be run as open shops, the listening workers jumped to their feet. They shouted in a protest that could be heard many blocks away: "Send it back, we will not consider it!" "We refuse to vote on it!" "We want recognition of the union!"

When the noise died down, one of the strikers stood and moved (put forth for a vote) that they send the proposal back to the manufacturers without any further discussion. The other strikers unanimously approved the motion. They would continue the strike until the factory owners agreed to recognize the union. The scene at the other meeting halls was much the same—the strikers all rejected the manufacturers' proposal. A striking worker at the Manhattan Lyceum expressed the thoughts of the crowd when she shouted from the gallery, "We'll be hungry unionists rather than well-fed scabs."

The strikers faced the New Year, 1910, with a resolve to hold out until their demand for union shops was met. It was the busy season in the shirtwaist trade, and the manufacturers needed the strike to end. The workers hoped the manufacturers would give up before they did.

CHAPTER 8

THE END
AND THE
BEGINNING

> There has been a tradition that women cannot strike. These young, inexperienced girls have proved that women can strike, and strike successfully."
>
> —Miriam Finn Scott, educator, 1910

The strike rolled into its seventh week in January 1910. After the strikers refused the manufacturers' proposal, the manufacturers refused to arbitrate (negotiate). As long as the strikers insisted on union recognition, the manufacturers' association said it could not meet the strikers' demands. Newspaper coverage of the strike lessened. As fewer and fewer articles appeared, enthusiasm and public support for the strike dwindled.

A RALLY AT CARNEGIE HALL

On January 2, 1910, the WTUL, the women's committee of the Socialist Party, the Equality League of Self-Supporting Women, and the National Woman Suffrage League organized a meeting at Carnegie Hall. Its purpose was to show support for the strike and to protest poor treatment of strikers by magistrates and police officers. A front-page notice in the *Call* urged anyone in sympathy with the strikers to

Some attendees thought that some of the speeches at the January 2, 1910, rally at Carnegie Hall in New York were too radical.

attend. Attendees would hear from young women who had served time in the workhouse for picketing—women who had learned firsthand that "the club is mightier than the constitution."

Carnegie Hall was decorated with banners that read, "A Striker Is Not a Criminal" and "Every One Has the Legal Right to Picket." Hundreds of strikers sat on the stage before a huge crowd. Women who had served sentences in the Blackwells Island workhouse wore sashes with bold black letters that read, "Workhouse Prisoner." Behind them, wearing sashes that read, "Arrested," sat 350 strikers who had been arrested for picketing. Alva Belmont and Anne Morgan sat in box seats with other wealthy strike sympathizers. Sprinkled throughout the hall were college women who supported the strike. The magistrates were invited. All but one declined to appear.

The speakers condemned the conduct of New York's public officials during the strike. "We are here because the weakest and most defenseless of our people have been denied the equal protection of the law," said attorney Miles Dawson. "We must take steps to compel the police and the Magistrates to give us that justice to which the law entitles us as citizens of this city."

Attorney Morris Hillquit, a prominent Socialist, received loud, hearty applause when he rose to speak. He took aim at factory owners and the brutish men they hired to harass the strikers. Then he condemned the magistrates. "There was no attempt even to administer justice," said Hillquit. "There was nothing but personal prejudice, personal vindictiveness, personal partisanship [loyalty]. The judges, and some of them expressed it very concisely, hoped by their harsh treatment to break the strikers' spirits and to break the strike. Vain, silly hopes. . . . This strike serves to demonstrate how deeply women have penetrated into the industrial life of our city and of our country, and that they not only know how to work as well as the men, but how to fight for their rights with the same energy, heroism, perseverance as the best men."

Hillquit stressed that the strike had to continue until employers agreed to hire only union workers. A strong union, he explained, would protect the workers from the greed of the manufacturers and give the workers power. If the employers granted all the strikers' other demands but did not recognize the union, shirtwaist factories would quickly revert to prestrike conditions—the same old industrial slavery. Hillquit went on to describe the strike as a struggle between the working class and the capitalist class, and his fiery speech worked on the emotions of the crowd. "Be of good cheer, sisters," he said in closing, "you are not alone in the struggle. Your fight is our fight, your cause is good, your fight is brave, your victory will be glorious."

Several of the strikers shared stories of their encounters with police on the picket lines and their experiences in

Morris Hillquit peppered his speech at Carnegie Hall with Socialist ideology.

court with New York's judges. Rose Perr told the story of her arrest and imprisonment. Leonora O'Reilly of the WTUL made a moving appeal for aid for the strikers. She said the strike had done more to make people of all classes "recognize their common bond of kinship than the preaching of all the churches and all the ethical schools had done in years." The crowd took up a collection to support the strikers.

■ DIVISION

For all the talk of how the strike was a unifying force for women, the Carnegie Hall rally was actually divisive. Some of the speakers had put forth a Socialist agenda. They saw the shirtwaist strike as part of a Socialist revolution—one that would lead to radical changes in U.S. society and the economy. This message shocked some women in the audience. They felt it was too extreme, too revolutionary. Yes, some individual police officers and judges had treated the strikers unfairly, but the entire social structure of the nation was not to blame, they said.

Many wealthy women who had supported the strike felt that Socialists were using the strikers as pawns. Anne Morgan expressed her feelings in the *New York Times.* "I am heartily in favor of the strikers," said Morgan, "and I believe they have been very badly treated by the courts. A protest along sane and reasonable lines was justifiable, but I deplore the appeals of Morris Hillquit, Leonora O'Reilly, and others. It is necessary to appeal to reason and sound judgment, but it was dangerous to allow this Socialistic appeal to emotionalism, and it is reprehensible for the Socialists to take advantage at this time to preach their fanatical doctrines." Morgan and several other wealthy women took a less active role in the strike after the Carnegie Hall meeting.

Morris Hillquit responded to Morgan's attack in the *Times* the following day:

> In this strike all supporters and sympathizers of the struggling shirtwaist makers, Socialists, trade unionists, settlement workers, suffragettes, and good people generally, have been working together harmoniously with the sole aim in view—to help the striking girls to victory. The movement has been entirely free from partisan [party-based] politics or controversies, and the attempt to introduce such controversies while the struggle is still in progress is, to say the least, rather injudicious [unwise]."

As the various factions argued in the press, the weary strikers continued their vigil on the picket lines. The union treasury was nearly empty. The strikers and the WTUL focused on raising money.

This illustration shows Anne Morgan talking to the press about the shirtwaist workers' strike. The alliance between the poor strikers and their wealthy supporters wasn't always smooth.

FUND-RAISING AND ROAD TRIPS

The New Amsterdam Theatre was one of many groups that agreed to help. It offered to give strikers 50 percent of the proceeds of all tickets sold for the play *The Barrier* during its three-week run in New York. The theater managers made it clear that they did not side with the strikers against the factory owners but merely wanted to help relieve the women's suffering. Meanwhile, shirtwaist makers whose shops had settled and who had returned to work collected dimes for the workers still out on strike. Rose Schneiderman appealed to the members of a Manhattan church to support the strikers, and the pastor took up a collection.

With about six thousand workers still out on strike, even benefits as low as two dollars a week for each striker quickly drained the strike fund. So WTUL members, college women, and striking shirtwaist makers traveled to women's colleges to raise more money. Violet Pike, Elsie Cole, and Rose Perr went to Poughkeepsie, New York, and spoke to a group of Vassar women. Rose Schneiderman traveled to Massachusetts. She spoke at parlor meetings and at Radcliffe College and Wellesley College. She spoke at historic Faneuil Hall in Boston and went to union meetings with Boston WTUL members. Schneiderman charged one hundred dollars for each appearance and donated her fee to the strike fund. From

Rose Schneiderman began working in a garment factory as a teenager and soon became a union leader.

Boston she stopped at every large town in New England and for four weeks slept in a different hotel every night. She raised ten thousand dollars for the strike fund, a small fortune at the time.

Pauline Newman had worked for the Triangle Waist Company when the strike began. In early 1910, she traveled around the state of New York. She went to Buffalo, Rochester, and Syracuse. During the day, she spoke to wealthy women's groups; at night, to union meetings. She described shop conditions in shirtwaist factories, the wages workers earned, and what led them to go on strike. Many who heard Newman contributed generously to the strike fund.

A DOWNHILL SLIDE

Both the strikers and the manufacturers were getting desperate. Salvatore Ninfo, a union organizer, traveled to Connecticut and Massachusetts to encourage shirtwaist makers in other towns and cities to go on strike. Alva Belmont suggested that all working women in the city of New York declare a "sympathy strike" to force the manufacturers to settle with the shirtwaist makers. Female school teachers declined to participate in Belmont's plan. "I do not believe a sympathetic strike of this kind would gain anything," said teacher Henrietta Rodman. "And nothing could compensate for the injury done the school children of the city by

PARIS FASHIONS

The WTUL encouraged its wealthy supporters to buy only union-made shirtwaists. But wealthy women didn't buy much ready-made clothing. For instance, Anne Morgan, one of the wealthiest women in the United States, often bought custom-made clothing from the finest fashion houses in Paris, France. The shirtwaists she purchased in Europe were not made by union workers.

the women teachers joining such a strike."

In early January, the New York State Board of Arbitration got involved in the dispute. This group was appointed by the governor to help resolve strikes. The board met with representatives from the manufacturers and the ILGWU. But negotiations broke down quickly. The union insisted that every factory hire only union workers, and the manufacturers refused to consider anything but an open shop.

In early February, an arbitration board in Philadelphia managed to settle the strike in that city. The factories there would operate as open shops. The workweek was set at fifty-two and a half hours, and the wage scale would be settled individually by each shop.

On February 7, Alva Belmont held a luncheon at Delmonico's Restaurant in New York City. Clara Lemlich, Anne Morgan, Mary Dreier, and other WTUL members attended the luncheon. So did teachers, society women, and manufacturers who had already settled with the union. Belmont brought the once-opposing parties together to soothe any lingering hostility caused by the strike.

Mary Dreier urged the women at the luncheon to wear only shirtwaists made by union workers. She hoped that women across the city would do the same. She said,

> If all the women in New York will agree to ask for and buy only shirtwaists with the union label, which shows that the manufacturer employs union workers, gives them fair pay, and makes the goods under decent and sanitary conditions, then the shops will have to supply goods with the union label, the manufacturers will have to comply with the conditions which will enable them to use them and the little girl shirtwaist makers will receive fair wages and satisfactory conditions.

The ambitious plan was not entirely successful. The teacher's association as a whole did not endorse it, although several individual teachers did promise to wear only union-made shirtwaists. Anne Morgan agreed that all the shirtwaists she purchased in the United States would contain the union label.

Charlotte Perkins Gilman was a prominent American writer, suffragist, and lecturer for social reform. In 1912 she wrote an anthem for the WTUL. Called "We Stand as One," the song declared:

Long have we lived apart,
Women alone;
Each with an empty heart,
Women alone;
Now we begin to see
How to live safe and free,
No more on earth shall be
Women alone.

Now we have learned the truth,
Union is power;
Weak and strong, age and youth,
Union is power;
On to the end we go,
Stronger our League must grow,
We can win Justice so,
Union is power!

For the right pay for us,
We stand as one;
For the short day for us,
We stand as one;
Loyal and brave and strong;
Helping the world along,
For end to every wrong
We stand as one!

Author and suffragist Charlotte Perkins Gilman is shown here in 1900.

By mid-February, most of the city's small and midsize factories—more than 350 shops—had settled with the union. Their strikers had returned to work under union contracts. But nineteen of the largest shirtwaist factories, including the Triangle Waist Company, remained firm in their demand for an open shop. They refused to sign union agreements. In addition, the Association of Waist and Dress Manufacturers did not recognize the union.

The strike gradually sputtered to a stop. The ILGWU came to believe that the shirtwaist workers had gained all they could gain from the strike. The union was ready to compromise. It accepted the manufacturers' December proposal, and factory owners agreed to give striking workers their jobs back. The owners did not agree to hire only union workers, however. The strike was declared officially over on February 15, 1910.

Physically weary and run-down, some on the brink of starvation, the shirtwaist makers were relieved to be back at work earning wages. WTUL and union leaders focused on what the strikers had gained from the strike rather than what they hadn't. Leaders then turned their attention to other sectors of the garment industry where working conditions also needed to be changed.

■ ■ ■ RESULTS OF THE STRIKE

So what did the strikers gain? Helen Marot said they had gained "more than half a loaf of victory." After the strike, shirtwaist factories operated on a fifty-two-and-one-half-hour workweek. Manufacturers paid overtime for hours worked above that total. They also provided four paid holidays a year. Each shop determined its own wage scale, and work was divided as equally as possible between all employees during the slow season. Manufacturers also agreed to furnish all needles, thread, and supplies needed for making shirtwaists. Some shops were unionized, although the largest shirtwaist factories remained open shops.

Those were the tangible results of the strike. But far more important, perhaps, were the intangible results—results that affected women in the years ahead. The shirtwaist strike laid the foundation for unionism in the garment industry. During the first year after the strike, Local 25 counted more than ten thousand members. "The girls in every trade are listening to suggestions of unionizing now," said Helen Marot. "The shirtwaist strike has been a tremendously educative [instructive] force." Unions grew strong throughout the garment industry. They worked to improve factory conditions wherever garments were made in the United States.

The young, immigrant shirtwaist makers had demonstrated that women—for the first time in U.S. history—could organize and bring about change in labor struggles. The strike was a turning point in the political power of the immigrant working class and a turning point for women as a whole. It proved that upper-class, middle-class, and working-class women could join together for political change. Women had emerged from the shadows and onto the public stage. They had become a force in the labor movement as well as in the broader political arena. The strike gave women political identities and set the stage for expanding women's rights. According to one article, written a month after the strike ended, the strike "revealed woman to herself as few incidents in history have done and in ways never to be forgotten."

The strike also pricked the nation's social conscience. According to Morris Hillquit, "The people of this city began to realize that society owes some duties to the toiling masses." The Uprising of

> **"The people of this city began to realize that society owes some duties to the toiling masses."**
> —Morris Hillquit, attorney for striking shirtwaist workers, January 1910

Twenty Thousand also sparked other, larger strikes within the garment industry. One of them took place just five months after the shirtwaist strike ended.

■ ■ ■ THE GREAT REVOLT OF 1910

On July 7, 1910, at two in the afternoon, sixty thousand cloak makers went on strike. "If girls can do it, why can't we?" asked one striker. The majority of cloak makers were men, and they walked out for the same reasons the shirtwaist makers had before them—to protest low pay, long hours, poor working conditions, charges for electricity and equipment, and an unfair subcontracting system. In contrast to the shirtwaist strike, this massive walkout, called the Great Revolt, was carefully planned in advance and well funded. When the cloak makers walked out, nearly the entire garment industry skidded to a standstill.

The strike lasted from July 7 until September 2. It ended with an agreement that altered unionism and labor relations in the United States and pushed the country toward an era of social reform. The agreement was called the Protocol of Peace. It applied to all workers in the garment industry, including shirtwaist workers. The agreement raised wages for garment workers, reduced working hours to fifty a week, eliminated charges and fines against employees, and abolished subcontracting.

The Protocol of Peace brought a new spirit of employer-employee cooperation to the garment industry. It also introduced several new concepts in labor relations. For instance, it established a Board of Sanitary Control to ensure adequate safety and sanitary conditions in factories. Board members, chosen by the ILGWU and the manufacturers, inspected garment factories in New York and monitored working conditions. The agreement also created ways for workers and owners to settle disputes. Minor disputes went before a committee on grievances. Major issues and minor ones that could not be settled by the committee on grievances went before a board of arbitration.

The Protocol of Peace also created a compromise on open versus closed shops. The agreement created a new classification called the preferential union shop. In this kind of shop, manufacturers gave

Women made up a small minority of cloak makers. However, in the Great Revolt of 1910, women played a prominent role in organizing and managing the strike. Union leaders appointed Helen Marot and Leonora O'Reilly to the cloak makers' strike committee.

preference in hiring to union workers, when they were equal in competence and experience to nonunion workers, but the hiring of nonunion workers was not forbidden.

Although the Protocol of Peace was a compromise, it represented a giant leap forward in the history of labor relations in the garment industry. Not all factory owners signed the Protocol of Peace, however.

CHAPTER 9

THE TRIANGLE FIRE

"We banded ourselves together, moved by a sense of stricken guilt, to prevent this kind of disaster from ever happening again."

—Frances Perkins, National Consumers League, after the Triangle Waist Company fire of 1911

After the shirtwaist strike and the Great Revolt, business returned to normal in New York's garment district. The shirtwaist workers went back to their shops, some of them with new union contracts. At the Triangle Waist Company, the owners had refused to recognize the union. They had also refused to sign the Protocol of Peace. As a result, conditions at Triangle were much the same in 1911 as they had been during the shirtwaist strike.

Triangle occupied the top three floors of the ten-story Asch Building on the corner of Washington Place and Greene Street. Under city fire codes, Triangle was considered fireproof. But the codes were very lax. The fire codes did not require factories to have sprinkler systems. Nor did they require fire drills for factory employees. The Triangle shop had one small fire escape that ended 5 feet (1.5 m) from the ground. It had a narrow stairway and two small passenger elevators on the Washington Place side of the building and a narrow stairway and two freight elevators on the Greene Street side.

THE EIGHTH FLOOR

The eighth floor held the factory's main cutting room. There, large stacks of fabric sat on long tables waiting to be cut into shapes. Tissue paper patterns dangled from wires over the tables. Young

The Asch Building in New York City housed the Triangle Waist Company on its top three floors.

male cutters were paid well for their skill at arranging the patterns on fabric, like pieces of a jigsaw puzzle, using the least yardage possible. The cutters sliced through the many layers of fabric with short knives and then piled the cut pieces in stacks, ready to be sewn into blouses. Large wooden scrap bins sat under the cutting tables, filled with hundreds of pounds of fabric and tissue paper scraps.

Five rows of sewing machines filled the rest of the eighth floor, separated by narrow aisles. Wicker baskets, piled high with garments, sat on the floor by each machine operator's feet. Stacks of finished garments waited for pickup by workers from the company's shipping department. Wooden partitions at the back of the room separated the work area from a cloakroom and restrooms.

On Saturday, March 25, 1911, about five hundred employees were at work in the Triangle shop. Most of them were young women between the ages of fourteen and twenty-three. It was payday and near quitting time, the end of a long week. The women and teenage girls chatted about their evening plans as they fastened on new spring hats and picked up coats and handbags from the cloakroom.

At 4:40 P.M., one of the cutters absentmindedly tossed a smoldering cigarette into a scrap bin. The paper and fabric in the bin immediately caught fire. Samuel Bernstein, the factory manager, and several cutters grabbed red fire buckets filled with water. They dumped the water on the flames, but the wooden bin had already ignited into an inferno. Combustible cloth, tissue paper, wooden tables and chairs, wicker baskets, and oil from the sewing machines spread the fire quickly.

The paper patterns caught fire, and burning wisps of flimsy cotton and paper swirled around the room. When they landed on the sewing and cutting tables, they touched off new flames, eager to devour the half-made blouses that cluttered the room. Some of the workers rushed to the Greene Street door and ran down the stairs to safety. Others ran to the Washington Place door and tried to get out that way. But the door swung inward instead of outward, and with dozens of women jammed against it, the door would not open. Thick black smoke swirled around the room, and flames soon reached the ceiling.

Louis Brown, a machinist, bullied his way through the crowd at the Washington Place door and yanked it open. Scores of terrified workers poured down the stairs. Others piled into the elevators and made it to safety. Still others left by the fire escape, but it was too narrow and rickety to hold more than a few people at a time. The narrow ladder led down into a courtyard, which quickly filled with smoke and fire. Seeing the fire below, a worker at the head of the fire escape line broke a window on the building's sixth floor. About twenty men and women crawled through the window into an empty workroom there, but others remained crowded on the fire escape. It soon crumbled from the heat and collapsed, carrying dozens of women to their deaths.

The twisted remains of a fire escape after the fire at the Asch Building

■■■■ ■ THE NINTH FLOOR

On the ninth floor, about 350 workers sat at eight long sewing tables that ran the width of the room. At first they had no warning that a fire had started one floor below. But the flames broke out windows, raced to the stairways, and shot up the building's airshaft, reaching the ninth floor within minutes and then the tenth. Soon all three floors of the Triangle Waist Company were engulfed in flames. The factory quickly became a furnace. The flames fought upward to the roof and then mushroomed back down.

On the ninth floor, as flames swept across the room, workers ran across tabletops, looking for a way out. Some screamed, choking on the thick smoke. Some fainted, overcome by the intense heat. "My sister Sarah and I worked alongside of each other and our cousin Josey worked a little ways off," said Tessa Benani. "We ran with about forty other girls to the Washington Place doors and found them locked, and we beat on those iron doors with our bare hands and tried to tear off the big padlock. The girls behind us were screaming and crying."

With the Washington Place door locked and fire cutting off the other exits, the workers on the ninth floor were trapped. Panic spread as quickly as the flames. A great cloud of black, billowing smoke forced the workers to the windows. They leaned out to gasp fresh air. The flames relentlessly followed, so workers stood on the ledge outside the windows as the flames licked at their feet.

Joseph Zito, an elevator operator, took his car up and down as quickly as he could in a mad rush to rescue the trapped workers. "When I'd made almost twenty trips, I could see as I started up for another load that the flames were spreading all across the elevator shaft at the eighth floor," he said. "I couldn't go up into that, and at any time the fire might burn out the top rests of the cable. So I started back to the street floor, and as I did there was an awful bang on the top of the elevator and blood dropped on me. It was a girl who had jumped down the shaft when she saw, I guess, that the elevator wasn't ever coming up again. And before I got to the bottom floor one body after another was slamming on top of the elevator cage."

The Triangle factory doors were frequently kept locked to keep workers from coming in late, leaving early, or taking unscheduled breaks. Locking doors was also a way to prevent theft. Fire insurance inspector Peter McKeon inspected the factory in 1909. "I even found that the door to the main stairway was usually kept locked," he said. "I was told that this was done because it was so difficult to keep track of so many girls. They would run back and forth between the floors, and even out of the building the managers told me." The fire inspector also noted that the workers were not given any fire drills or instructions about what to do in case of fire. On McKeon's recommendation, H. F. J. Porter, an industrial engineer, contacted Triangle's owners and offered to conduct fire drills for their employees. Blanck and Harris never acknowledged his letter.

THE TENTH FLOOR

Triangle owners Max Blanck and Isaac Harris had their offices on the tenth floor. The tenth floor also held the business's showrooms, the pressing department, and the packing department. Two of Max Blanck's six children, twelve-year-old Henrietta and five-year-old Mildred, were visiting their father at the factory with their French governess that day. After work, Blanck had promised to take the girls shopping.

Isaac Harris led the workers on the tenth floor through the smoke-filled stairway to the roof. In the building next door, part of New York University, law professor Frank Sommer and twenty-five students heard breaking glass and screaming coming from the Asch Building. They ran to the roof of the university building and found two ladders left by painters the previous day. The law school building was one story taller than the Asch Building, but Sommer and his students rigged a makeshift bridge out of the ladders, placed it between the two buildings, and then helped the Triangle workers crawl across the ladders to safety. About seventy people escaped this way, including Isaac Harris, Max Blanck, his two children, and their governess.

■ ■ ■ A SCENE OF HORROR

On the streets around the Asch Building, hundreds of New Yorkers had been enjoying the spring day, strolling or lounging in Washington Square. Trees were budding, and the breeze was mild. The tranquil setting changed in an instant. The Triangle windows shattered, and glass rained down on the placid group below. Black smoke billowed out from the eighth floor. A bystander pulled a nearby fire alarm box. Before long, clanging red fire wagons pulled by powerful horses rolled into the square from every direction. The fire wagons arrived mere minutes after the alarm sounded. The first police officers on the scene were from the Mercer Street Station, the station that had held so many pickets during the shirtwaist strike.

Horse-drawn fire engines race down the street on their way to the Triangle fire.

Firefighters spray water toward the upper floors of the Asch Building on March 25, 1911.

The sound of the fire trucks brought people out of nearby shops and restaurants, and bystanders quickly filled the sidewalks. They saw fire and smoke in the Triangle windows. Then a large dark bundle fell from one of the windows. The people on the street thought the factory owner was tossing out his best fabric, trying to save his merchandise. Then another bundle fell. And another. And the bystanders realized that the bundles were human beings—women and teenage girls who had leaped to their deaths to keep from being burned alive.

Firefighters and police officers frantically tried to help the frightened workers. They raised their ladders to rescue young women from window ledges. But the ladders were too short. They reached only to the sixth floor, 30 feet (9 m) below the trapped women. The officers

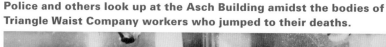

Police and others look up at the Asch Building amidst the bodies of Triangle Waist Company workers who jumped to their deaths.

stretched out nets and blankets to catch the young women plunging out of windows. But their bodies hit with such force that they tore through the nets and onto the sidewalk. They jumped in twos and threes, often with their clothes or hair on fire. They lay on the sidewalk in piles, as water from the firefighters' hoses rained down on them. William Shepherd, a reporter for the United Press, described the scene as he watched from a pay phone across the street:

> I learned a new sound, a more horrible sound than description can picture. It was the thud of a speeding, living body on a stone sidewalk. Thud—dead, thud—dead, thud—dead, thud—dead. There was plenty of chance to watch them as they came down. The height was eighty feet [24 m]. The first ten thud—deads, shocked me. I looked up, saw that there were scores of girls at the windows. The flames from the floor below were beating in their faces. Somehow I knew that they, too, must come down. I even watched one girl falling, waving her arms, trying to keep her body upright, until the very instant she struck the sidewalk. Then came the thud—then a silent, unmoving pile of clothing, and twisted, broken limbs.

"I learned a new sound, a more horrible sound than description can picture. It was the thud of a speeding, living body on a stone sidewalk. Thud—dead, thud—dead, thud—dead, thud—dead. There was plenty of chance to watch them as they came down."

—William Shepherd, reporter for the United Press, on people jumping from windows during the Triangle fire, March 1911

■ ■ ■ ■ THE MORGUE

In less than half an hour, the fire was out. Firefighters and police officers entered the building and began their ghastly search. On the ninth floor, they found piles of charred remains of bodies. Women had huddled together in groups by the stairways, doors, and elevator shafts, cut off by the flames. After looking at one corpse, a reporter asked a police officer if it was male or female. "It's human," he said, "that's all you can tell."

Thousands of New Yorkers had seen the plumes of black smoke in the sky and gathered on the streets around the Asch Building. Some were friends or family members of Triangle workers, looking for their loved ones. Others were drawn to the scene, appalled, yet unable to tear themselves away. "The floods of water from the firemen's hoses that ran into the gutter were actually red with blood," said William Shepherd. "I looked upon the heap of dead bodies and I remembered these girls were the shirtwaist makers. I remembered their great strike of last year in which these same girls had demanded more sanitary conditions and more safety precautions in the shops. These dead bodies were the answer."

The ninth floor of the Asch Building after the fire

Firefighters lower the body of a victim of the fire at the Triangle Waist Company to the street below.

Firefighters removed the bodies from the street and placed them in pine coffins. Bodies from the ninth floor were lowered down to the street by ropes. Emergency workers numbered each coffin. Anything that could help identify a body—rings, watches, handbags, broken combs, gloves, and bits of clothing—was placed with it in the coffin. Workers loaded the coffins onto patrol wagons and ambulances for the trip to the city morgue. But the morgue was too small to hold all the dead, so the city set up a temporary morgue at Manhattan's Charities Pier. The dead numbered 146: 123 women and girls and 23 men. The youngest victim was a fourteen-year-old girl. It was the greatest loss of life in a workplace disaster in New York up to that time.

Morgue workers propped up the corpses in open coffins and lined

Family members and friends walk through the morgue after the Triangle fire to identify their missing loved ones in this detail of a photograph.

them up in rows. For a week, mothers, fathers, sisters, brothers, cousins, and sweethearts walked slowly down the long rows of coffins and identified their loved ones. When a body was claimed, family members took the coffin to be buried. Some bodies were so badly burned that identification was impossible. A ring with the initials Y.G. was the only way Yetta Goldstein's family could identify her—a young woman who had been arrested several times during the shirtwaist strike. By the end of the week, only seven bodies remained unclaimed.

A CITY MOURNS

After the fire, many people remembered the shirtwaist strike. They realized that some of the dead workers were the same ones who had fought for better working conditions the year before. People felt they knew the young women who had died, and they took their deaths personally. New Yorkers were outraged. They believed that the fire would not have robbed their community of so many lives if Triangle's owners had listened to the strikers when they tried to improve conditions in the factory. Many people also felt guilty—guilty for not demanding safe factories.

The Red Cross, the ILGWU, and the WTUL formed a relief committee to provide financial relief for victims' families. People of all social classes donated money, including $5,000 from wealthy industrialist Andrew Carnegie. Even small children gave to the cause. Collections totaled more than $120,000.

Most of the victims had lived from week to week and supported their families on their factory wages. Some had been the primary wage earners for their families. Their deaths left these families desperate. WTUL volunteers visited victims' homes to determine individual needs. In some cases, the relief fund paid funeral expenses. In others, it gave money to families whose primary wage earner had been lost in the fire. The fund also sent money to Europe for the support of foreign dependents of the victims.

Industrialist Andrew Carnegie was one of many wealthy New Yorkers who gave money to help the families of fire victims.

Meanwhile, accusations flew from all quarters, as people tried to fix blame. New Yorkers believed that someone was responsible. Whether it was the city building department, the state labor commission, the fire department, building owner Joseph Asch, or Triangle bosses Max Blanck and Isaac Harris—someone was guilty and needed to be punished. Scores of city officials inspected the Asch Building and

(Left to right) Coroner Holzhauser and Assistant District Attorneys J. Robert Rubin and Charles Bostwick investigate the roof of the Asch Building after the 1911 fire.

conducted four separate investigations. "The conditions as they now exist are hideous and damnable," said Lillian Wald, a member of the Board of Sanitary Control. "Our investigations have shown that there are hundreds of buildings which invite disaster just as much as did the Asch structure."

New Yorkers held protest rallies and memorial meetings all over the city. At a meeting at Cooper Union, Morris Hillquit called for social change:

> The girls who went on strike last year were trying to readjust the conditions under which they were obliged to work. I wonder if there is not some connection between that fire and that strike. I wonder if our Magistrates who sent to jail the girls who did picket duty in front of the Triangle shop realized last Sunday that some of the responsibility may be theirs. Had that strike been successful those girls might have been alive today and the citizenry of New York would have less of a burden upon its conscience.

On April 2, Anne Morgan rented the Metropolitan Opera House for a memorial and protest meeting sponsored by the WTUL. The speakers at the meeting demanded better fire protection laws for factories. Rabbi Stephen Wise, one of the speakers, placed responsibility for the fire on human greed—greed that compelled factory owners to place profits above human life. He held the entire city responsible for allowing the unsafe conditions to exist. "The lesson of the hour," he said, "is that while property is good, life is better; that while possessions are valuable, life is without price. Because life is sacred we realize to-day the indivisible oneness of human welfare. These women and these men will have died in vain unless we to-day highly resolve that my brother's wrong is my wrong."

The emotions of the packed crowd were raw. Listeners interrupted the speakers with shouts and hisses, and the meeting threatened to break up into chaos. The audience's anger spilled over into a demand for radical change. Then Rose Schneiderman calmed the frenzied crowd. She spoke, barely above a whisper. "I would be a traitor to these poor burned bodies," she said, "if I came here to talk good fellowship. We have tried you good people of the public and we have found you wanting."

Three days later, an estimated four hundred thousand mourners lined the streets of New York in a drenching rain for the funeral procession of the seven unidentified workers killed in the fire. A huge line of black-clad mourners formed behind flower-covered hearses. Mary Dreier and Helen Marot of the WTUL walked on either side of Rose Schneiderman. Survivors of the fire, as well as family members and friends of the victims, marched in a silent procession. When the

Labor union members gather to mourn the loss of life in the Triangle Waist Company fire in New York City.

procession reached Washington Square and the Asch Building, the mourners poured out their sorrow. According to the *American* magazine, "It was one long-drawn-out, heart-piercing cry, the mingling of thousands of voices, a sort of human thunder in the elemental storm—a cry that was perhaps the most impressive expression of human grief ever heard in this city." The unidentified victims were buried in the Evergreen Cemetery in Brooklyn, New York.

> "It was one long-drawn-out, heart-piercing cry, the mingling of thousands of voices, a sort of human thunder in the elemental storm—a cry that was perhaps the most impressive expression of human grief ever heard in this city."
>
> —American *magazine article about the funeral procession for the Triangle fire victims, April 1911*

THE AFTERMATH

Blame finally settled on Triangle owners Max Blanck and Isaac Harris. On April 11, 1911, District Attorney Charles Whitman charged them with manslaughter. The case hinged on evidence that in violation of the law, the Washington Place door on the Asch Building's ninth floor had been locked. The body of twenty-two-year-old Margaret Schwartz, along with scores of other charred remains, was found behind the door. The district attorney attempted to prove that Schwartz had tried to escape through the door, could not, and had died as a direct result of the locked door.

Blanck and Harris hired attorney Max D. Steuer, considered by many to be the greatest trial lawyer in New York. The trial began on December 4, 1911, and lasted three weeks. The case centered on whether the door had been locked, whether Blanck and Harris knew it had been locked, and whether Margaret Schwartz would have survived had the door been open. Judge Thomas Crain charged the jury with specific instructions for reaching a verdict. Not only did the evidence have to prove that the door had been locked and that the defendants had known it, but the jury also had to find that Schwartz had died as a result of that locked door.

In the end, the jury acquitted Blanck and Harris of responsibility for the locked door. The owners then proceeded to collect their insurance money, rent another building, and continue making shirtwaists in conditions much like those in their former factory. Two years later, the authorities arrested Max Blanck for locking workers into his new factory during the workday. He was tried, found guilty, and fined twenty dollars.

■ ■ ■ REFORM

The Triangle fire brought New Yorkers together emotionally and spiritually. It galvanized the city into action and led to resolve that a similar horror would not happen again. Three months after the fire, New York governor John Alden Dix signed a bill that created the Factory Investigating Commission. Led by future senator Robert Wagner and future governor Al Smith, the committee investigated factory safety all over the state of New York.

The governor appointed Mary Dreier of the WTUL to the commission. Frances Perkins of the National Consumers League and union activists Rose Schneiderman, Pauline Newman, and Clara Lemlich were part of the team of investigators. They went on a statewide tour of factories to assess working conditions in more than twenty industries. Their investigation included fire safety but went beyond that to examine the general conditions of factory life and how they affected workers.

The commission investigated thousands of factories over four years. It took testimony from fire inspectors, health officials, and labor leaders, and more than two hundred witnesses testified during the

Led by future New York governor Al Smith, the Factory Investigating Commission evaluated working conditions in many types of factories in New York State. In addition to fire safety, the commission investigated working conditions for women and children, sanitation, accident prevention, industrial poisoning, and disease. The commission's aim was the preservation of human life.

first year alone. The commission's findings led to new laws to protect factory workers: eight the first year, twenty-five the following year, and three in 1914.

The new laws affected every aspect of factory life. Factory owners were required to provide automatic sprinkler systems in high-rise buildings, doors that opened outward and were kept unlocked during working hours, and fire drills for employees. Factories also had to have adequate lighting, ventilation (air movement), and washrooms. Women could not work more than fifty-four hours a week, and children under the age of fourteen could not work in factories at all. Reform began in New York and spread to other states. One by one, legislatures across the United States enacted new laws to protect the nation's workers.

■ ■ ■ ■ LEGACY

The Uprising of Twenty Thousand was a pivotal moment in U.S. labor history, and the Triangle fire finished what the strike had begun. The shirtwaist strike focused the nation's attention on working conditions in factories and created a desire for change. The Triangle fire spurred the nation to action. After the strike and fire, labor unions grew in number, power, and size. Reforms that the strikers had fought for were enacted all across the country.

But the struggle for workers' rights was far from over. In the following years, U.S. labor unions continued to organize, strike, and bargain with business owners. They experienced many setbacks, but they also won many victories.

The Uprising of Twenty Thousand was also a pivotal moment for women in the United States. During the strike, Jewish, Italian, and native-born women, from the poorest slum dwellers to the richest society matrons, joined together in a common cause. Women crossed ethnic and class lines to bring about change. In 1920 they finally won the right to vote through the Nineteenth Amendment to the U.S. Constitution. In the following years, women found a new voice in the workplace, in the political arena, and on the world stage. The shirtwaist workers strike sowed the seeds for all these changes.

1880–1920: More than twenty-three million immigrants come to the United States.

1886: The American Federation of Labor (AFL) forms to protect the interests of skilled workers.

1900: The International Ladies Garment Workers Union (ILGWU) forms in New York.

1903: The Women's Trade Union League (WTUL) forms to support trade unionism.

1906: Shirtwaist makers form a union, Local 25 of the ILGWU.

1909:

September Shirtwaist makers from the Triangle Waist Company and the Leiserson Shirtwaist Company go on strike.

November 23 New York shirtwaist makers declare a general strike.

Late November Factory owners form the Association of Waist and Dress Manufacturers of New York in an attempt to break the strike.

December 3 Strikers march to city hall and present a formal protest to the mayor about the unfair arrest of pickets.

December 5 Strikers and their supporters attend a meeting at the Hippodrome Theatre.

December 15 Strike supporters hold a fund-raiser at the Colony Club.

December 20 Philadelphia shirtwaist workers join the strike.

1910:

January 2	Striking shirtwaist workers hold a rally at Carnegie Hall.
Early February	The shirtwaist strike ends in Philadelphia.
February 15	The shirtwaist strike ends in New York.
July 7	New York cloak makers go on strike.
September	Union leaders and factory owners sign the Protocol of Peace.

1911:

March 25	A fire at the Triangle Waist Company kills 146 workers.
April 5	Four hundred thousand mourners attend the funeral of seven unidentified workers killed in the Triangle fire.
June 30	New York State creates the Factory Investigating Commission to improve factory safety.
December	Triangle owners Max Blanck and Isaac Harris are tried and acquitted of manslaughter in the Triangle fire.

1920: The Nineteenth Amendment to the U.S. Constitution gives women the right to vote.

Alva Smith Vanderbilt Belmont

(1853–1933) Belmont was born on January 17, 1853, in Mobile, Alabama. From an early age, she demonstrated her belief that girls and boys were equals. When she was a child, Alva climbed a tree to pick apples. After a boy called to her that girls could not climb trees, Alva scurried down the tree and beat up the boy. Alva's family moved to New York when she was seven years old. She also lived in Paris, France, for a few years. During the shirtwaist strike, Belmont organized legal aid for the strikers and appeared in court with arrested pickets. She paid their bail and court fees and contributed money to the strike fund. Belmont also financed several meetings and rallies, including the Hippodrome meeting and an automobile picket parade. Belmont was an ardent suffragist and women's rights activist. She founded the Political Equality Association and sponsored suffrage meetings at Marble House, her Newport, Rhode Island, mansion. In 1922 she donated money for the purchase of the National Woman's Party headquarters in Washington, D.C., and became the group's president.

Mary Dreier

(1875–1963) Dreier was born into a wealthy family in Brooklyn, New York. She joined the WTUL because she wanted to work for an important cause. Dreier served as president of the WTUL from 1907 to 1914 and remained active in the organization until 1950. Arrested during the shirtwaist strike, she became a leading spokesperson for labor reform for female workers. Governor John Alden Dix appointed her to the Factory Investigating Commission after the Triangle fire. In this job, she helped to write a report that led to new labor laws to protect factory workers.

Morris Hillquit

(1869–1933) Hillquit was born in 1869 in Riga, Latvia, then part of the Russian Empire. He came to New York when he was seventeen years old, lived with his family in a tenement on the Lower East Side, and worked in a garment factory. He earned a law degree from New York University and wrote several books on Socialism. A leader of the Socialist Party, Hillquit became an active union organizer and helped found the United Hebrew Trades, a garment workers' union. During the shirtwaist strike, he defended many arrested pickets in court. He also worked on the relief committee to help distribute funds to victims' families after the Triangle fire. Hillquit ran unsuccessfully for U.S. Congress five times and for mayor of New York twice.

Clara Lemlich

(1886–1982) Lemlich was born in Gorodok, Ukraine, in 1886. As a girl, she helped her mother run a small grocery store and made buttonholes for tailors in her village. She used her earnings to buy books, some of which taught her the revolutionary doctrines of Socialism. Clara's family emigrated from Ukraine to the United States in 1905. They settled in New York. Although Clara wanted to go to school, she began work in a shirtwaist factory to help support her family. In 1906 Clara was one of seven women and six men to form Local 25 of the ILGWU. She worked tirelessly for the shirtwaist strike and was beaten by police and arrested several times. After the strike, Lemlich joined the Socialist Party and worked for woman suffrage.

Theresa Malkiel

(1874–1949) Malkiel was born in Russia. She arrived in New York in 1891, when she was seventeen years old. She began work in a cloak-making factory, became an ardent Socialist, and dedicated herself to improving working conditions for women. Along with her husband, she founded the *Call*, New York's leading Socialist newspaper. Malkiel was a member of the executive board of the WTUL and a member of the shirtwaist strike committee. She wrote many articles and pamphlets supporting the strike. She also worked for woman suffrage and promoted adult education for immigrant women.

Helen Marot

(1865–1940) Marot was born in Philadelphia, Pennsylvania. Her parents were wealthy Quakers, members of a religious group that promotes simplicity, pacifism (opposition to war and violence), and equality for all people. Marot worked as a librarian and opened a private library with materials on social reform. A writer, Socialist, and trade unionist, Marot wrote several books on labor topics and many articles about the shirtwaist strike. Her writing shed light on labor issues from the workers' point of view. As secretary of the WTUL, Marot also worked to eliminate child labor and improve working conditions for men and women. She was committed to organizing labor as a whole, rather than organizing women as a separate group.

Anne Morgan

(1873–1952) The youngest daughter of wealthy financier J. Pierpont Morgan, Anne was born in Highland Falls, New York. Athletic as a child, Anne grew up in her family's mansions in New York, Great Britain, and France. She relaxed on yachts and wore custom-made clothing from the finest fashion houses in Paris. As an adult, she crisscrossed the world with her father. She and two wealthy friends built the Colony Club in New York as a private women's club, complete with a swimming pool and squash courts. Morgan supported the shirtwaist strike financially and in the press. She invited the strikers to the Colony Club to share their stories with society women.

Pauline Newman

(ca. 1890–1986) Newman was born in Kovno, Lithuania. Her exact year of birth is not known. As a Jewish girl in Lithuania, Pauline's educational options were limited. She was not allowed to attend public school because she was Jewish and poor. The local religious school admitted only boys. Newman's resentment at this inequality sparked her desire to work to end sex discrimination. Pauline and her family emigrated from Lithuania to New York in 1901. There, Newman joined the Socialist Literary Society and learned English. She began work at the Triangle Waist Company in October 1901 and worked until the strike in 1909. She played a key role in organizing and sustaining the strike. She traveled around New York, spoke to groups of women, and raised money for the strikers. She also spoke extensively about women's suffrage. After the Triangle fire, she took lawmakers on tours of New York factories and worked to improve factory safety standards.

Leonora O'Reilly

(1870–1927) The daughter of Irish immigrants, O'Reilly was born in New York City. Her father died when she was a year old, and her childhood on the Lower East Side was one of stark poverty. Her mother was a shirtwaist worker. When Leonora was a small child, her mother often carried her to union meetings. Leonora began sewing collars in a shirtwaist factory when she was thirteen years old. In 1886 she helped form the Working

Women's Society. Organized to support working women and promote laws for factory safety, the group educated the public about working conditions for wage-earning women. Their efforts resulted in the country's first factory inspection law. O'Reilly sat on the executive board of the WTUL. She was active in the shirtwaist strike and the woman suffrage movement. She was also a member of the Socialist Party and a founding member of the National Association for the Advancement of Colored People.

Frances Perkins

(1880–1965) Perkins was born in Boston, Massachusetts. She attended Mount Holyoke College and Columbia University. Perkins was active in the labor, social reform, and women's suffrage movements. She was a witness to the Triangle fire of 1911. Deeply moved by the tragedy, she worked harder than ever to improve working conditions for women. She became a key investigator on the Factory Investigating Commission and later became the industrial commissioner of New York. In 1933 President Franklin D. Roosevelt appointed Perkins U.S. secretary of labor, making her the first woman in the United States to hold a cabinet (presidential advisory) post. As secretary of labor, Perkins wrote key legislation for unemployment relief, the minimum wage, the abolition of child labor, and Social Security.

Rose Schneiderman

(1882–1972) Schneiderman was born to Jewish parents in Poland. She came to the United States in 1890 and lived with her family on the Lower East Side. Her father died two years later, and Rose and her brothers went to live in an orphanage for a time. She entered the labor force at the age of thirteen as an errand girl at a department store. She earned $2.16 a week for sixty-four hours of work. After a few years, she found a job at a cap factory making linings for men's caps. Schneiderman was famous for her fiery speeches and flame red hair. She was a passionate advocate for trade unionism, feminism, and Socialism. During the shirtwaist strike, she marched on picket lines and taught the strikers the principles of trade unionism. She also traveled extensively on behalf of the strikers, speaking at meetings and assembly halls to raise money for their support. Schneiderman worked for the WTUL, the ILGWU, and the New York Woman Suffrage Party.

Rose Pastor Stokes

(1879–1933) Stokes was born in Augustow, Poland. She moved to Cleveland, Ohio, in 1890. At the age of thirteen, she began work in a cigar factory. She worked at the factory for twelve years, for much of the time as the sole supporter of a family of six. An avid reader, Stokes saw a call for articles for the *Jewish Daily News* and became a regular contributor to the paper. The editor of the newspaper offered her a full-time job as a journalist, so Rose and her family moved to New York. During the shirtwaist strike, Stokes passed out thousands of ribbons to the strikers. The ribbons bore her slogan: "Starve to win, or you'll starve anyway." Stokes was also an ardent suffragist, a Socialist Party leader, a birth control advocate, and a staunch advocate for the working class.

arbitration: a process by which impartial individuals attempt to resolve a dispute

capitalism: an economic system characterized by the private ownership of business, with little government regulation of pricing, production, and the distribution of goods

closed shop: a factory that can employ only union workers

general strike: an organized work stoppage across an entire industry

open shop: a factory that can employ union and nonunion workers

picket: to protest in front of a place of employment during a labor strike

scab: a slang name for a strikebreaker

Socialism: an economic system in which the government strictly regulates business and distributes wealth equally among all citizens

strike: an organized work stoppage by employees, designed to force employers to accept workers' demands for higher wages and better working conditions

strikebreaker: a person who works at a factory where the employees are out on strike

subcontracting: a system whereby an employer hires another employer, who in turn hires a group of workers to complete a job

suffrage: the right to vote

sweatshop: a small factory in which employees work for long hours, at low wages, and in unsafe conditions

sympathy strike: a strike undertaken to support another group of strikers

tenement: a run-down apartment building with substandard sanitation, safety, and comfort

union: an organization of workers united to fight for better wages and working conditions

5   William Mailly, "Working Girls' Strike Result of Oppression," *New York Call*, December 29, 1909, 1.

6   *New York Times*, "40,000 Called Out in Women's Strike," November 23, 1909, 16.

7   *New York Call*, "30,000 Waist Makers Declare Big Strike," November 23, 1909, 1.

7   Louis Levine, *The Women's Garment Workers: A History of the International Ladies' Garment Workers' Union* (New York: B. W. Huebsch, 1924), 154.

8   Sue Ainslie Clark and Edith Wyatt, "Working-Girls' Budgets: The Shirtwaist-Makers and Their Strike," *McClure's*, November 1910, 81.

10 Susan A. Glenn, *Daughters of the Shtetl: Life and Labor in the Immigrant Generation* (Ithaca, NY: Cornell University Press, 1990), 88.

12 National Park Service, "Statue of Liberty National Monument and Ellis Island," nps.gov, June 28, 2006, http://www.nps.gov/archive/stli/prod02.htm (February 11, 2009).

13 Leonard Covello, *The Social Background of the Italo-American School Child* (Totowa, NJ: Rowman and Littlefield, 1972), 265.

15 Ibid., 235.

15 Sydelle Kramer and Jenny Masur, eds., *Jewish Grandmothers* (Boston: Beacon Press, 1976), 125.

16 PBS. "Gallery: Millionaire's Row, the Frick Mansion," *American Experience*, 2009, http://www.pbs.org/wgbh/amex/carnegie/gallery/frickman.html (February 21, 2009).

20 Elias Tcherikower, ed., *The Early Jewish Labor Movement in the United States* (New York: Yivo Institute for Jewish Research, 1961), 119.

21 Nan Enstad, *Ladies of Labor, Girls of Adventure* (New York: Columbia University Press, 1999), 53.

22 Rose Cohen, *Out of the Shadow: A Russian Jewish Girlhood on the Lower East Side* (Ithaca, NY: Cornell University Press, 1995), 71.

22 Elizabeth Ewen, *Immigrant Women in the Land of Dollars: Life and Culture on the Lower East Side, 1890–1925* (New York: Monthly Review Press, 1985), 68.

24 Abraham Cahan, *The Imported Bridegroom and Other Stories of the New York Ghetto* (1898; rep., New York: Garrett Press, 1968), 166.

24 Ewen, 100.

25 Sadie Frowne, "The Story of a Sweatshop Girl," *Independent*, September 25, 1902, 2,281.

25 Joel Seidman, *The Needle Trades*, Labor in Twentieth Century America series (New York: Farrar & Rinehart, 1942), 37.

26 Barbara Mayer Wertheimer, *We Were There: The Story of Working Women in America* (New York: Pantheon Books, 1977), 294.

28 Pauline Newman, "Letters to Michael and Hugh from P. M. Newman," May 1951, in *The Triangle Factory Fire*, Kheel Center, Cornell University ILR School, March 2, 2002, http://www.ilr.cornell.edu/trianglefire/texts/letters/newman_letter.html?location=Sweatshops+and+Strikes (March 6, 2009).

28 *New York Call*, "Waist Strike Story Told to Rich Women," December 16, 1909, 2.

28 Leon Stein, ed., *Out of the Sweatshop* (New York: Quandrangle, 1977), 66.

28 "The Power and the People (1898–1914)," *New York: A Documentary Film*, episode 4, DVD, directed and written by Ric Burns (Arlington, VA: PBS, 1999).

30   Clark and Wyatt, 72.

31   Frowne, 2,282.

31   Wertheimer, 294.

31   Rose Schneiderman, *All for One* (New York: Paul S. Eriksson, 1967), 86–87.

32   Frowne, 2,282.

33   Stein, *Out of the Sweatshop*, 66.

33   *New York Call*, "Waist Strike Story," 2.

36   Theresa Malkiel, "The Jobless Girls," *New York Call*, December 29, 1909, 2.

39   Miriam Finn Scott, "The Spirit of the Girl Strikers," *Outlook*, February 19, 1910, 392.

39   *New York Sun*, "40,000 Work Girls at Ease," November 30, 1909, 1.

40   Stein, *Out of the Sweatshop*, 66.

41   *New York Times*, "Girl Strikers Well Treated, Says Baker," November 6, 1909, 3.

41   *New York Sun*, "40,000 Work Girls," 1.

42   Ibid.

43   Clark and Wyatt, 81.

44   Helen Marot, "A Woman's Strike–An Appreciation of the Shirtwaist Makers of New York" *Proceedings of the Academy of Political Science in the City of New York*, October 1910, 126.

44   Malkiel, "The Jobless Girls," 2.

45   *New York Call*, "Will Expose Waist Bosses at Meeting," December 13, 1909, 2.

45   *New York Call*, "7,000 Waist Makers Win Speedy Victory," November 25, 1909, 2.

45   *New York Call*, "2,000 More Waist Makers Victorious," November 26, 1909, 1.

45   *New York Call*, "Hillquit Bares Waist Bosses' Nefarious Plot," December 14, 1909, 1–2.

46   *New York Times*, "Suffragists to Aid Girl Waist Strikers," December 2, 1909, 3.

47   *New York Times*, "Waist Strike Grows," November 25, 1909, 20.

47   *New York Times*, "Girl Strikers Dance as Employers Meet," November 28, 1909, 3.

48   *New York Times*, "Girl Strikers Riot; Quelled by Police," November 27, 1909, 3.

48   *New York Call*, "Waist Strike Story," 2.

48   *New York Times*, "Arrest Strikers for Being Assaulted," November 5, 1909, 1.

49   *New York Times*, "To Arbitrate Waist Strike," December 11, 1909, 3.

49   Scott, "The Spirit of the Girl Strikers," 397.

49   *New York Call*, "7,000 Waist Makers," 1.

50   Clark and Wyatt, 82.

50   Ibid.

50   Schneiderman, 94.

50   Clark and Wyatt, 82.

51–52 *New York Times*, "Pickets from Prison Are Guests of Honor," December 23, 1909, 7.

53   Philip S. Foner, *Women and the American Labor Movement: From Colonial Times to the Eve of World War I* (New York: Free Press, 1979), 327.

53   Marot, 126.

54   Ibid.

56   International Ladies' Garment Workers' Union, "The Uprising of the Twenty Thousands," in *Let's Sing!*, available online at Kheel Center, Cornell University ILR School, The Triangle Factory Fire, March 2, 2002, http://www.ilr.cornell

.edu/trianglefire/texts/songs/
uprising.html (February 5,
2009).

56 *New York Times,* "Girl Strikers Go
to the City Hall," December 4,
1909, 20.

58–59 Ibid.

60 Linda Gordon Kuzmack, *Woman's
Cause: The Jewish Woman's Movement
in England and the United States, 1881–
1933* (Columbus: Ohio State
University Press, 1990), 142.

61 Schneiderman, 121.

62 *New York Times,* "Parson's Flings
Stir Suffragettes," February 6,
1910, 4.

62 Irving Howe, *World of Our Fathers*
(New York: Harcourt Brace
Jovanovich, 1976), 299.

62–63 *New York Times,* "Strikers Divide
on Suffrage," December 3, 1909,
6.

63 *New York Sun,* "Suffrage and
Shirtwaists," December 2, 1909,
1.

64 *New York Times,* "Suffragists to Aid
Girl Waist Strikers," December
2, 1909, 3.

64 Schneiderman, 118, 121.

64 *New York Sun,* "One Grand
Feminine Sob," November 26,
1909, 1.

64 *New York Times,* "Suffragists to Aid
Girl Waist Strikers," 3.

64–65 *New York Call,* "Waistmakers
Winning in New York and
Philadelphia Despite Police
Persecution," December 23,
1909, 2.

65 *New York Sun,* "Shirtwaist Strike to
Go On," December 14, 1909, 1.

66–67 *New York Sun,* "Mrs. Belmont's Girl
Dreams," November 7, 1909, 1.

67 *New York Times,* "Calls Waist Strike
Anarchy," January 20, 1910, 18.

69 *New York Times,* "Throng Cheers

on the Girl Strikers," December
6, 1909, 1.

69 Ibid.

69 *New York Sun,* "Throng to Cheer
for Women," December 6, 1909,
1.

70 *New York Times,* "Throng Cheers,"
1.

70 *New York Sun,* "Throng to Cheer,"
2.

72 Ibid.

72 *New York Times,* "Won't Arbitrate
Shirtwaist Strike," December 12,
1909, 5.

73 *New York Call,* "7,000 Waist
Makers," 2.

74 Charlotte Baum, *The Jewish Woman
in America* (New York: New
American Library, 1975), 121.

75 *New York Times,* "Mrs. Gaynor
Admits She's a Suffragist,"
December 30, 1909, 9.

75 *New York Times,* "Miss Morgan
Aids Girl Waiststrikers,"
December 14, 1909, 1.

77 *New York World,* "Mrs. Belmont
and Miss Morgan Are to Direct
Strike," December 20, 1909, 1.

77–78 *New York Call,* "Waist Makers
of New York City Cheered by
Philadelphia Strike," December
21, 1909, 2.

78 *New York Call,* "Waistmakers'
Union through the Call Denies
That the Strike Is about to Be
Called Off," December 25, 1909,
1.

78 *New York World,* "Mrs. Belmont
and Miss Morgan," 2.

79 *New York Call,* "Waist Makers of
New York City," 2.

79 *New York Tribune,* "Mrs. Belmont
Helps," December 19, 1909, 1.

79 *New York Times,* "Church to the
Aid of Girl Strikers," December
20, 1909, 1.

81 New York Times, "Girl Strikers Tell the Rich Their Woes," December 16, 1909, 3.

81 Ibid.

82 New York Times, "Police Break Up Strikers' Meeting," December 22, 1909, 8.

83 New York Times, "Autos for Strikers in Shirtwaist War," December 21, 1909, 1.

83 Nancy Schrom Dye, As Equals and as Sisters: Feminism, the Labor Movement, and the Women's Trade Union League of New York (Columbia: University of Missouri Press, 1980), 92.

83 New York Times, "The Shirtwaist Strike: Its Merits Are Obscured by the Notoriety Seekers," December 16, 1909, 8.

83–84 New York Sun, "Watchers to Aid Strikers," December 20, 1909, 1.

85 New York Times, "Critical Time for Shirtwaist Strike," December 15, 1909, 8.

86 New York Times, "Ida Tarbell with Strikers," January 16, 1910, 1.

88 New York Times, "Police Mishandle Girl Strike Pickets," December 10, 1909, 13.

88 New York Times, "Mrs. Belmont Aids Arrested Strikers," December 19, 1909, 1.

88 New York World, "Graduate of Vassar in 'Pen' Nine Hours," December 20, 1909, 2.

88 Ibid.

89 William A. McKeever, "Is Your Daughter Safe at College?" New York Times Magazine, March 20, 1910, SM10.

90 New York Times Magazine, "College Girls as Pickets in a Strike," December 19, 1909, SM5.

90 Ibid.

90 Ibid.

90 Ibid.

91 New York Times, "Miss Taft to Aid the Girl Strikers," January 16, 1910, 1.

91 New York Times, "Bryn Mawr Girl Tells Prison Story," January 31, 1910, 1.

91 New York Times, "Bryn Mawr Student in Jail," January 30, 1910, 1.

91 New York Times, "Bryn Mawr Girl Tells Prison Story."

92 New York Times, "Facing Starvation to Keep Up Strike," December 25, 1909, 2.

92 Mary Clark Barnes, "The Strike of the Shirtwaist Makers," The World To-Day: A Monthly Record of Human Progress, March 1910, 267.

93 New York Times, "Critical Time," 8.

94 Mailly, 2.

94 New York Call, "Girls Sell 'Strike Special' of the Call," December 30, 1909, 1.

95 Ibid., 2.

96 Ibid.

96 New York Times, "Shirtwaist Strike Peace Plan Fails," December 28, 1909, 5.

96 New York Call, "Waist Makers Unanimously Reject the 'Open Shop' Offer of the Manufacturers," December 28, 1909, 1.

97 Ibid.

98 Miriam Finn Scott, "What the Women Strikers Won," Outlook, July 2, 1910, 480.

100 New York Call, "On to Carnegie Hall Tomorrow!" January 1, 1910, 1.

100 New York Call, "370 Arrested Waist Strikers on Platform at Carnegie Hall," January 3, 1910, 1.

100   New York Times, "The Rich Out to Aid Girl Waistmakers," January 3, 1910, 1.

100   New York Call, "370 Arrested," 2.

101   Ibid.

101   New York Times, "The Rich," 1.

102   New York Times, "State Arbitrators in Girls' Strike," January 4, 1910, 20.

102   New York Times, "Strike Funds Low; Arbitration Fails," January 5, 1910, 20.

105–106   New York Times, "Mrs. Belmont Wants All-Woman Strike," January 8, 1910, 5.

106   New York Times, "Mrs. Belmont to Buy Only Union Waists," February 8, 1910, 5.

107   Charlotte Perkins Gilman, "We Stand as One," Life and Labor, May 1912, 153.

108   New York Times, "Shirtwaist Girls Say They Won Strike," March 8, 1910, 2.

109   Ibid.

109   Barnes, 268.

109   Ibid.

109   Foner, 344.

110   Kuzmack, 125.

112   "The Power and the People (1898–1914)," New York: A Documentary Film.

116   Martha Bensley Bruere, "The Triangle Fire," Life and Labor, May 1911, 138.

116   New York Sun, "141 Dead in Factory Fire," March 26, 1911, 1.

117   New York Times, "Lack of Fire Drill Held Responsible," March 26, 1911, 5.

121   "The Power and the People (1898–1914)," New York: A Documentary Film.

121   Ibid.

122   New York Times, "141 Men and Girls Die in Waist Factory Fire," March 26, 1911, 1.

122   Leon Stein, The Triangle Fire (Ithaca, NY: ILR Press, 1962), 20.

128   Ibid, 121.

128   New York Times, "Public Indifference Held Responsible," April 1, 1911, 3.

128   New York Times, "Mass Meeting Calls for New Fire Laws," April 3, 1911, 3.

129   Ibid.

130   Stein, Triangle Fire, 152–153.

130   Ibid.

Baum, Charlotte. *The Jewish Woman in America*. New York: New American Library, 1975.

Baxandall, Rosalyn, and Linda Gordon, eds. *America's Working Women: A Documentary History 1600 to the Present*. New York: W. W. Norton and Company, 1995.

Cahan, Abraham. *The Imported Bridegroom and Other Stories of the New York Ghetto*. 1898. Reprint, New York: Garrett Press, 1968.

Coan, Peter Morton. *Ellis Island Interviews: In Their Own Words*. New York: Facts on File, 1997.

Cohen, Adam. *Nothing to Fear*. New York: Penguin Press, 2009.

Cohen, Rose. *Out of the Shadow: A Russian Jewish Girlhood on the Lower East Side*. Ithaca, NY: Cornell University Press, 1995.

Covello, Leonard. *The Social Background of the Italo-American School Child*. Totowa, NJ: Rowman and Littlefield, 1972.

Diner, Hasia R., and Beryl Liefe Benderly. *Her Works Praise Her: A History of Jewish Women in America from Colonial Times to the Present*. New York: Basic Books, 2002.

Downey, Fairfax. *Portrait of an Era as Drawn by C. D. Gibson*. New York: Charles Scribner's Sons, 1936.

Dubinsky, David. *David Dubinsky: A Life with Labor*. New York: Simon and Schuster, 1977.

Dublin, Thomas, ed. *Immigrant Voices: New Lives in America 1773–1986*. Urbana: University of Illinois Press, 1993.

Dye, Nancy Schrom. *As Equals and as Sisters: Feminism, the Labor Movement, and the Women's Trade Union League of New York*. Columbia: University of Missouri Press, 1980.

Enstad, Nan. *Ladies of Labor, Girls of Adventure*. New York: Columbia University Press, 1999.

Ewen, Elizabeth. *Immigrant Women in the Land of Dollars: Life and Culture on the Lower East Side, 1890–1925*. New York: Monthly Review Press, 1985.

Flexner, Eleanor, and Ellen Fitzpatrick. *Century of Struggle: The Woman's Rights Movement in the United States*. Cambridge, MA: Belknap Press of Harvard University Press, 1959.

Foerster, Robert F. *The Italian Emigration of Our Times*. New York: Arno Press, 1969.

Foner, Philip S. *Women and the American Labor Movement: From Colonial Times to the Eve of World War I*. New York: Free Press, 1979.

Glenn, Susan A. *Daughters of the Shtetl: Life and Labor in the Immigrant Generation*. Ithaca, NY: Cornell University Press, 1990.

Green, James R. *The World of the Worker: Labor in Twentieth-Century America*, Urbana: University of Illinois Press, 1980.

Hasanovitz, Elizabeth. *One of Them: Chapters from a Passionate Autobiography*. Boston: Houghton Mifflin Company, 1918.

Hindus, Milton, ed. *The Jewish East Side 1881–1924*. New Brunswick, NJ: Transaction Publishers, 1996.

Homberger, Eric. *The Historical Atlas of New York City*. New York: Henry Holt and Company, 1994.

Hoobler, Dorothy, and Thomas Hoobler. *The Italian American Family Album*. New York: Oxford University Press, 1994.

Howe, Irving. *World of Our Fathers*. New York: Harcourt Brace Jovanovich, 1976.

Hunter, Robert. *Poverty*. New York: Macmillan Company, 1904.

Hyman, Paula E., and Deborah Dash Moore, eds. *Jewish Women in America*. 2 vols. New York: Routledge, 1997.

Iorizzo, Luciano J. *The Italian Americans*. Boston: Twayne Publishers, 1980.

Jensen, Joan M., and Sue Davidson, eds. *A Needle, a Bobbin, a Strike*. Philadelphia: Temple University Press, 1984.

Kramer, Sydelle, and Jenny Masur, eds. *Jewish Grandmothers*. Boston: Beacon Press, 1976.

Kuzmack, Linda Gordon. *Woman's Cause: The Jewish Woman's Movement in England and the United States, 1881–1933*. Columbus: Ohio State University Press, 1990.

Laslett, John, and Mary Tyler. *The ILGWU in Los Angeles 1907–1988*. Inglewood, CA: Ten Star Press, 1989.

Leeder, Elaine. *The Gentle General: Rose Pesotta Anarchist and Labor Organizer*. New York: State University of New York Press, 1993.

Levine, Louis. *The Women's Garment Workers: A History of the International Ladies' Garment Workers' Union*. New York: B. W. Huebsch, 1924.

Malkiel, Theresa S. *The Diary of a Shirtwaist Striker*. Ithaca, NY: ILR Press, 1910.

McClymer, John F. *The Triangle Strike and Fire*. Forth Worth, TX: Harcourt Brace College Publishers, 1998.

Metzker, Isaac, ed. *A Bintel Brief: Sixty Years of Letters from the Lower East Side to the Jewish Daily Forward*. New York: Schocken Books, 1971.

Morrison, Joan, and Charlotte Fox Zabusky. *American Mosaic: The Immigrant Experience in the Words of Those Who Lived It*. Pittsburgh: University of Pittsburgh Press, 1980.

National American Woman Suffrage Association. *Woman Suffrage: Arguments and Results*. New York: National American Woman Suffrage Association, 1910.

Newcomer, Mabel. *A Century of Higher Education for American Women*. New York: Harper and Brothers Publishers, 1959.

Odencrantz, Louise C. *Italian Women in Industry: A Study of Conditions in New York City*. New York: Russell Sage Foundation, 1919.

Parmet, Robert D. *The Master of Seventh Avenue: David Dubinsky and the American Labor Movement*. New York: New York University Press, 2005.

Perun, Pamela J. *The Undergraduate Woman: Issues in Educational Equity*. Lexington, MA: Lexington Books, 1982.

Riis, Jacob A. *How the Other Half Lives*. New York: Dover Publications, 1971.

Sachar, Howard M. *A History of the Jews in America*. New York: Alfred A. Knopf, 1992.

Schneiderman, Rose. *All for One*. New York: Paul S. Eriksson, 1967.

Seidman, Joel. *The Needle Trades*. Labor in Twentieth Century America series. New York: Farrar and Rinehart, 1942.

Sorin, Gerald. *A Time for Building: The Third Migration 1880–1920*. Baltimore: Johns Hopkins University Press, 1992.

Stein, Leon, ed. *Out of the Sweatshop*. New York: Quandrangle, 1977.

———. *The Triangle Fire*. Ithaca, NY: ILR Press, 1962.

Stolberg, Benjamin. *Tailor's Progress: The Story of a Famous Union and the Men Who Made It*. Garden City, NY: Doubleday, Doran and Company, 1944.

Stuart, Amanda Mackenzie. *Consuelo and Alva Vanderbilt*. New York: HarperCollins, 2005.

Tax, Meredith. *The Rising of the Women*. New York: Monthly Review Press, 1980.

Tcherikower, Elias, ed. *The Early Jewish Labor Movement in the United States*. New York: Yivo Institute for Jewish Research, 1961.

Tyler, Gus. *Look for the Union Label: A History of the International Ladies' Garment Workers' Union*. Armonk, NY: M. E. Sharpe, 1995.

Von Drehle, David. *Triangle: The Fire That Changed America.* New York: Grove Press, 2003.

Wagenknecht, Edward. *Daughters of the Covenant: Portraits of Six Jewish Women.* Amherst: University of Massachusetts Press, 1983.

Wertheimer, Barbara Mayer. *We Were There: The Story of Working Women in America.* New York: Pantheon Books, 1977.

Wolensky, Kenneth. *Fighting for the Union Label: The Women's Garment Industry and the ILGWU in Pennsylvania.* University Park: Pennsylvania State University Press, 2002.

Books

Auch, Mary Jane. *Ashes of Roses*. New York: Henry Holt and Company, 2002. In this historical novel for young readers, sixteen-year-old Rose Nolan emigrates from Ireland to New York City. She finds a job—but it is at the infamous Triangle Waist Factory, site of the horrific 1911 fire.

De Angelis, Gina. *The Triangle Shirtwaist Company Fire of 1911*. Philadelphia: Chelsea House Publishers, 2001. This title tells the story of not only the tragic Triangle fire of 1911 but also the Uprising of Twenty Thousand two years before. The author explains how female shirtwaist workers bolstered the growing labor movement in the garment trades.

Edge, Laura B. *Andrew Carnegie: Industrial Philanthropist*. Minneapolis: Twenty-First Century Books, 2004. This biography of Andrew Carnegie, the Scottish-born industrialist who made his fortune in the American railroad and steel businesses, details Carnegie's life and business dealings. It also covers Carnegie's philanthropy, including his support of education and libraries in the early twentieth century.

Houle, Michelle M. *Triangle Shirtwaist Factory Fire: Flames of Labor Reform*. Berkeley Heights, NJ: Enslow Publishers, 2002. The author tells the horrifying story of the tragic 1911 fire at the Triangle Waist Factory. She explains the conditions that led up to the fire and some of the reforms that followed it.

Kendall, Martha E. *Failure Is Impossible! The History of American Women's Rights*. Minneapolis: Twenty-First Century Books, 2001. This title in the People's History series chronicles the movement for women's rights in the United States. The author examines women's fight for property rights, voting rights, reproductive rights, and more.

Richards, Marlee. *America in the 1910s*. Minneapolis: Twenty-First Century Books, 2010. This book in the Decades of Twentieth-Century America series covers all aspects of life in the 1910s in the United States, including the women's suffrage movement.

Skurzynski, Gloria. *Sweat and Blood: A History of U.S. Labor Unions*. Minneapolis: Twenty-First Century Books, 2009. This comprehensive title documents the history of the labor movement in the United States—from the colonial era to modern times. Black-and-white illustrations and photos complement the text.

Websites

America 1900

> http://www.pbs.org/wgbh/amex/1900/
> This website, a companion to the film of the same name, presents a vivid picture of life in the United States at the turn of the twentieth century. The website offers compelling images, documents, and stories of ordinary people. It includes material on technological advances, women's changing roles in society, and the immigrant experience.

Ellis Island

> http://www.ellisisland.org
> This website provides historical information about Ellis Island—a major immigrant reception center in New York City—and the immigrant experience. The site includes immigration statistics by date and country of origin. Visitors can even search for relatives who immigrated to the United States through Ellis Island.

Heaven Will Protect the Working Girl: Immigrant Women in the Turn-of-the-Century City

> http://www.ashp.cuny.edu/video/heaven/index.html
> Designed for use by teachers and students, this website provides a viewer's guide to the film of the same name. The site includes classroom activities; a timeline; and information on immigration history, labor history, women's history, and progressive reform.

The Triangle Factory Fire

> http://www.ilr.cornell.edu/trianglefire
> This website contains comprehensive information on the shirtwaist strike and the Triangle fire. The site includes primary source documents related to the fire and information on the investigation and trial of Triangle factory owners Max Blanck and Isaac Harris. The site also describes reforms enacted as a result of the fire and gives links to related websites.

owners of, 41, 55; refuses to settle strike, 108, 113; workers strike, 5, 35, 39. *See also* Triangle Factory fire

union contracts, 45
union label, 106
union negotiators, 45, 96
unions. *See* labor unions
United Press, report on Triangle fire, 121
Uprising of Girls, 9. *See also* strike, shirtwaist makers'
Uprising of Twenty Thousand, 9, 109–110; legacy of, 132–133. *See also* strike, shirtwaist makers'
U.S. Constitution: Nineteenth Amendment, 133; right to picket, 41

Valesh, Eva McDonald, 92
Vanderbilt, William K., 76
Vassar College students, 78, 87
violence, strike-related, 27, 50 52
vote, women's right to. *See* suffrage, woman

wages, garment workers', 5, 27, 33, 41, 47; after strike, 108
Wagner, Robert, 131
Wald, Lillian, 128
Waldorf Astoria, 94
Wall Street, 94
Washington Heights, 94

watchers, 78
wealth, industrial, 76
weather, 44, 53, 56, 92–93
"We Stand as One," 107
Wellesley College students, 87
Whitman, Charles, 130
women, immigrant, 13, 15, 109; roles of 15; work and, 15, 23, 27
women's colleges, 89
women's rights, 109, 133, 141. *See also* suffrage, woman
Women's Shirtwaist and Garment Makers' Union of Philadelphia, 85
Women's Trade Union League (WTLU), 6, 38–39, 49, 106, 136; anthem of, 107; dues to join, 38; marches on city hall, 56–58; mourns victims of fire, 129; president of, 80
workhouse, 49, 92
working conditions, garment workers', 5, 24–25, 27–28, 33; after strike, 108–111, 126; after Triangle fire, 131–132
working hours, 24, 27–28, 108
WTUL. *See* Women's Trade Union League (WTUL)
Wyatt, Edith, 49
Wyoming and woman suffrage, 62

Yiddish, 7

PHOTO ACKNOWLEDGMENTS

The images in this book are used with the permission of: © Brown Brothers, pp. 4, 5, 7, 11, 14, 16 (both), 20, 20–21, 30–31, 32, 42, 57, 58–59, 61, 66–67, 68, 76, 80, 82, 90, 115, 120, 123; The International Ladies Garment Workers Union Archives, Kheel Center, Cornell University, pp. 8–9, 28, 52, 55, 87, 94–95, 104, 113, 122, 124–125, 127; © Photodisc/Getty Images, p. 12; Library of Congress, pp. 17 (LC-D401-12683), 19 (LC-D4-36489), 23 (LC-DIG-nclc-04080), 25 (LC-DIG-nclc-04455), 34 (LC-DIG-hec-05183), 40 (LC-USZ62-41877), 48 (LC-USZ62-53517), 65 (LC-USZ62-103738), 70 (LC-DIG-hec-05374), 71 (LC-USZ62-16530), 75 (LC-USZ62-98999), 77 left (LC-DIG-ggbain-15196), 77 right (LC-DIG-ggbain-18322), 84 (LC-USZ62-48418), 107 (LC-USZ62-106490), 118 (LC-USZ62-34985), 126 (LC-USZ62-48403); © Laura Westlund/Independent Picture Service, p. 18; © W. and D. Downey/Hulton Archive/Getty Images, p. 29; Milstein Division of United States History, Local History & Genealogy, The New York Public Library, Astor, Lenox and Tilden Foundations, pp. 37, 51; © Museum of the City of New York/Byron Collection/Getty Images, pp. 38, 99; © Mary Evans/Pharcide/The Image Works, p. 93; © UnderwoodArchives.com, p. 101; © Mary Evans Picture Library/The Image Works, p. 103; © Keystone/Hulton Archive/Getty Images, p. 119; AP Photo/National Archives, File, pp. 128–129.

Cover: © Brown Brothers.

ABOUT THE AUTHOR

Laura B. Edge attended the University of Texas and studied educational concepts and philosophies at the American Institute of Foreign Study in London, Paris, Rome, and Athens. She has been a middle-school teacher and a computer programmer and trainer. She is the author of a biography of Andrew Carnegie, among other books, and lives in Kingwood, Texas, with her husband and two sons.